Becoming ~ ̂
Justice

This important book helps school leaders let go of a "comfortable" mindset and enter a world of courageous conversations that examine and challenge the impact of racism and other forms of oppression on disciplinary patterns, instructional practices, and school policies. Authors Hunsberger, Mayo, and Neal prepare you to address these difficult issues though authentic, critical discourse. The book includes classroom activities and facilitation tips to help prompt systematic changes in schools through improving instruction, supporting inclusiveness, and strengthening student engagement.

After reading *Becoming a Social Justice Leader*, you'll be able to:

- Design conversations that support participant engagement and create a safe environment for discussion.
- Explore personal dispositions, attitudes, and stances that contribute to systemic oppression.
- Understand how oppression is established and sustained in order to enact change.
- Create alliances within school settings to foster dialogue and combat oppression.

Additional worksheets that help educators examine and expand their work as social justice leaders are also available for download (www.routledge.com/9781138957749).

Phil Hunsberger is co-owner of Educational Equity Consultants and has served as a teacher, principal, and central office administrator.

Billie Mayo is co-owner of Educational Equity Consultants and former Assistant to the Deputy Superintendent of the St. Louis Public Schools.

Anthony Neal is President and CEO of Educational Equity Consultants and Adjunct Professor in the Communications Department at Webster University.

Other Eye On Education Books Available from Routledge
(www.routledge.com/eyeoneducation)

Five Critical Leadership Practices: The Secret to High-Performing Schools
Ruth C. Ash and Pat H. Hodge

Mentoring is a Verb: Strategies for Improving College and Career Readiness
Russ Olwell

How to Make Data Work: A Guide for Educational Leaders
Jenny Grant Rankin

A School Leader's Guide to Implementing the Common Core: Inclusive Practices for All Students
Gloria Campbell-Whatley, Dawson Hancock, and David M. Dunaway

Hiring the Best Staff for Your School: How to Use Narrative to Improve Your Recruiting Process
Rick Jetter

What Connected Educators Do Differently
Todd Whitaker, Jeffrey Zoul, and Jimmy Casas

BRAVO Principal! Building Relationships with Actions that Value Others, 2nd Edition
Sandra Harris

Get Organized! Time Management for School Leaders, 2nd Edition
Frank Buck

The Educator's Guide to Writing a Book: Practical Advice for Teachers and Leaders
Cathie E. West

Data, Data Everywhere: Bringing All The Data Together for Continuous School Improvement, 2nd Edition
Victoria Bernhardt

Leading Learning for Digital Natives: Combining Data and Technology in the Classroom
Rebecca J. Blink

Becoming a Social Justice Leader

Using Head, Heart, and Hands to Dismantle Oppression

Phil Hunsberger, Billie Mayo, and Anthony Neal

Routledge
Taylor & Francis Group

NEW YORK AND LONDON

First published 2016
by Routledge
711 Third Avenue, New York, NY 10017

and by Routledge
2 Park Square, Milton Park, Abingdon, Oxon, OX14 4RN

Routledge is an imprint of the Taylor & Francis Group, an informa business

© 2016 Taylor & Francis

Library of Congress Cataloging-in-Publication Data
Names: Hunsberger, Phil, author.
Title: Becoming a social justice leader : using head, heart, and hands to dismantle
    oppression / by Phil Hunsberger, Billie Mayo, and Anthony Neal.
Description: New York, NY ; London : Routledge, 2016. | Includes bibliographical
    references.
Identifiers: LCCN 2015033982| ISBN 9781138957725 (hardback) |
    ISBN 9781138957749 (pbk.) | ISBN 9781315661575 (e-book)
Subjects: LCSH: Social justice—Study and teaching. | Critical pedagogy. |
    Teaching—Social aspects.
Classification: LCC LC192.2 .H86 2016 | DDC 370.11/5—dc23
LC record available at http://lccn.loc.gov/2015033982

ISBN: 978-1-138-95772-5 (hbk)
ISBN: 978-1-138-95774-9 (pbk)
ISBN: 978-1-315-66157-5 (ebk)

Typeset in Optima
by Apex CoVantage, LLC

Contents

eResources

Many of the tools in this book can be downloaded and printed for classroom use. You can access these downloads by visiting the book product page on our website: www.routledge.com/9781138957749. Click on the "eResources" tab and select the files. They will begin downloading to your computer.

Foreword

On August 9, 2014, we lost another African American youth, Michael Brown, who was killed by a police officer in Ferguson, MO. His tragic death was a catalyst which propelled the Black Lives Matter campaign, "a rallying cry for ALL Black Lives striving for liberation," into a national movement.[1] We are continuing to witness the tragedy of more unarmed Black people being killed by police officers in Staten Island, NY, Beavercreek, OH, Los Angeles, CA, Cleveland, OH, Madison, WI, Charleston, SC, and Baltimore, MD.[2] For some we have watched the videos of their deaths go viral. Those images and the pain in the families' eyes and the anger and frustration of the protestors are now ingrained in our individual memory and part of the collective U.S. historical memory about race and racism.

Many of us are struggling with what to do, and how to address racism, especially anti-Black racism. As a resident of Baltimore City, I have been part of many discussions since the death of Freddie Gray[3] on how to "fix it." Lots of different solutions have been shared: addressing police brutality, creating more jobs for youth, tackling segregated housing, and investing in changes to the educational system. The ideas of "how to fix it" are being replicated in these communities and others. Some, many of whom are People of Color, are wondering: will it be different *this* time?

And we also know there are some residents in these communities who see no bias or ill intent, just police officers doing their jobs; or do not see these as incidents about race but as issues of the perceived crime rate in neighborhoods of color; or see this as an issue of poverty, complete with all the stereotypes that accompany that perception; or that it is about being a good parent, and assume that the "Baltimore mom" video that went viral[4] was about parenting and not about a mom in fear for her Black son's life being in danger; or assume the person's death was based on the victim's past regressions as the sole reason or major contributing factor to his/her death. Yet as Ta-Nehisi Coates shares in his book, *Between the World and Me*, this is indeed a story about racism. "Americans believe in the reality of 'race' as a defined, indubitable feature of the natural world. Racism—the need to ascribe bone-deep features to people and then humiliate, reduce, and destroy them—inevitably follows from this inalterable condition."

And race and place do matter; they are intertwined. To understand that reality is to begin to understand structural racism.[5] Any ZIP code in the U.S. will tell a story of one's life expectancy and how race and place are irrefutably linked in ways which can predict a person's life outcomes (in education, health, or interaction with the criminal justice system). We also know that race is intertwined with how the U.S. was created from the stolen indigenous land we live on, to colonialism, to enslaving Africans and others, to the Jim Crow period, to who could be educated and who could not, to who could be in the same classroom, and to our persistent inequitable resource distribution to schools based on property taxes.

So race and specifically racism is an important starting point for any conversation we want to have about how we each can be a social justice leader. I have learned over the years, while building the capacity of organizations and communities to align their policies, practices and culture with their value of equity, that it is helpful for the learning process to focus on racism first. After understanding the framework of racism, an organization can more readily focus on other "isms": sexism, classism, heterosexism, ableism, etc. Every form of oppression is tangled together and they reinforce each other. Though there is a similar architect, we know there is a specific story for each oppression that needs to be told and addressed. We also know when we are working in groups and focus across the board on all "isms," we find each "ism" can be diluted, or there can even be a competition between "isms." By focusing on racism, we can do the necessary critical dive by increasing our conceptual analysis and building the skills that are transferable to different "isms." Then once this framework is in place, each organization and community can more readily build its intersectional analysis so we can truly transform our systems to be equitable.

This leads us forward to this book, *Becoming a Social Justice Leader: Using Head, Heart, and Hands to Dismantle Oppression,* an evidence-based professional development program which shares a process, tools, and a well-tested curriculum for participants to lead change efforts within educational systems. Especially now, though it has been true always, we need educational professionals to be social justice advocates—it is a critical skill set and it is a responsibility. Participants in the Leadership and Racism program are now creating more equitable hiring practices, courageously engaging colleagues to discuss racism, creating more effective learning opportunities, especially for children of color, and much more to integrate the principles of equity within each district.

As we consider this hopeful tectonic shift for many U.S. residents' hearts and minds, public school systems are at a dynamic intersection to demand communities ensure equity for *all* of our children. The racial disparities in the U.S. are well known by most,[6] and it is obvious we need our best thinking, our change agent skills, to guarantee that each district's policies, practices, and culture reflect the educational goals of inclusion and equity. In many communities there has been progress, through institutional changes like implementing a multicultural curriculum and instruction, eliminating racial disparities in discipline policies and enforcement, providing students with English as second language instruction, engaging students, parents, and guardians as full partners in educational equity practices, and/or ensuring safe and quality facilities have been made. Yet the work is not always sustained.

As we work on transforming school districts, it is important for us not to work in an institutional vacuum. To address how discipline policy is implemented means we are working with police in the schools and their discretionary decision-making, with the child welfare system to address its policies, and with the juvenile justice system to assess the presence of implicit bias in its adjudication process. To ensure safe and quality facilities, we need to work with the community on current formulas of resource allocation to schools, and address housing segregation. To provide students, parents, and guardians with ESL instruction, we also need to work on immigration legislation. Our systemic focus is critical as social justice advocates working on educational change. Our plan needs to envision community change, not just institutional change. It needs to envision a different way of doing things that address power, it needs to envision policy change along with healing, and it needs to envision our linked fate for the next seven generations.

> We can and must get to the place where we all see ourselves as one movement, rather than as a collection of movements working in solidarity with one another. It's a subtle shift, but one that would serve us well. Being one movement doesn't mean we have to lose the specificity of our experiences and solutions, but it does mean that we can engage in a level of joint analysis, planning, and

action that would make the most of each community's assets. I can tell you, the leaders and foot soldiers of a single movement talk to each other far more often than do the leaders and foot soldiers of allied movements. . . . Martin Luther King, Jr., wrote in his *Letter from a Birmingham Jail*, "We are caught in an inescapable network of mutuality, tied in a single garment of destiny. Whatever affects one directly, affects all indirectly." There is a modern expression of this most fundamentally moral concept, and inserting that idea into the body politic is our own generation's responsibility.

Rinku Sen, Executive Director,
Race Forward and Publisher, Colorlines.com

Each school district is accountable to the community for building a quality educational foundation for each young person as well as their understanding of their connection and responsibility to the greater community. The school system's alignment of its policies, practices, and culture with equity and its transparency and communication with the community are critical and can be a model for other sectors within the community. The residents are also accountable to the school district for a consistent commitment to ensure each child in his or her community has access, tools, and quality instructional support to achieve their actual best. This book is well timed; it provides a roadmap on how educational professionals can develop their muscles to be the instigators and leaders in the community's journey for educational equity.

Maggie Potapchuk, MP Associates
July, 2015

Notes

1. "#BlackLivesMatter was created in 2012 after Trayvon Martin's murderer, George Zimmerman, was acquitted for his crime, and dead 17-year-old Trayvon was post-humously placed on trial for his own murder. Rooted in the experiences of Black people in this country who actively resist our de-humanization, #BlackLivesMatter is a call to action and a response to the virulent anti-Black racism that permeates our society. Black Lives Matter is a unique contribution that goes beyond extrajudicial killings of Black people by police and vigilantes." www.blacklivesmatter.com, accessed 7/17/15.

2. The following people were unarmed and were killed by police: Eric Garner, Staten Island New York, July 17, 2014; John Crawford III, Beavercreek, Ohio, August 5, 2014; Ezell Ford, Los Angeles, California, August 11, 2014; Taneisha Anderson, Cleveland, Ohio, November 13, 2014; Tamir Rice, Cleveland, Ohio, November 22, 2014; Anthony Robinson, Madison, Wisconsin, March 6, 2015; Walter Scott, Charleston, South Carolina, April 4, 2015; and Freddie Gray, Baltimore, Maryland, April 19, 2015.

3. "On April 12, 2015, Freddie Carlos Gray, Jr., a 25-year-old African-American man, was arrested by the Baltimore Police Department for possessing what the police alleged was an illegal switchblade. While being transported in a police van, Gray fell into a coma and was taken to a trauma center. Gray died on April 19, 2015; his death was ascribed to injuries to his spinal cord. On April 21, 2015, pending an investigation of the incident, six Baltimore police officers were temporarily suspended with pay." https://en.wikipedia.org/wiki/Death_of_Freddie_Gray, accessed July 17, 2015.

4. See Joan Walsh, The hideous white hypocrisy behind the Baltimore "Hero Mom" hype: How clueless media applause excuses police brutality, *Salon;* http://www.salon.com/2015/04/29/the_hideous_white_hypocrisy_ behind_the_baltimore_%E2%80%9Chero_mom%E2%80%9D_hype_ how_clueless_media_applause_excuses_police_brutality/, accessed July 18, 2015.

5. The definition of structural racism is located at: http://www.racialequity tools.org/glossary#structural-racism

6. For a list of racial disparities in different issue areas see: http://www.racia lequitytools.org/fundamentals/data#FUN17

Acknowledgments

We wish to acknowledge a number of individuals over the past decade who have provided us knowledge, experience, and the impetus leading to this manuscript. First and foremost, our appreciation is extended to the countless individuals who have joined us over the years in these courageous conversations. Though it may have been us serving as facilitators, their stories and the willingness to share have been gifts for us as *learners*. Much like that of the light bulb, there were dozens of inventers besides Thomas Edison that led to the product. Therefore, our work in the past has been with the National Conference of Community and Justice (NCCJ) of St. Louis. We served with others on the faculties of the Dismantling Racism Institute and the Dismantling Racism Institute for Educators sponsored by NCCJ. We, therefore, wish to acknowledge these individuals as they too served as "inventors" for our work: Maggie Potapchuk, Reggie Williams, Rudy Nickens, Leon Sharp, Mary Ferguson, Alia Mubarak Tharpe, Carmen Garcia, Jeannette Mott Oxford, Maxine Birdsong, Linda Holtzman, Mike McGrath, Deborah Holmes, Martin Rafanan, Charisse Jackson, Ron Hill, Rita Hill, Janet Katzengburg, Karen Cogan. We were able as well to work with Jarrod Schwartz, Executive Director of Just Communities, Santa Barbara, California. Mark McGrath serves our company as our fiscal agent, and his efforts to keep us afloat are much appreciated. We also extend a very special thanks to Peter Wilson whose dedication and expertise created Educational Equity Consultants and who served as our partner for numerous years as our programs began to build.

Certainly our appreciation is extended to our families for their support as well as their willingness *to read, re-read, and re-read yet again* as we worked on this manuscript. Educational Equity Consultants is located in St. Louis, Missouri. We have a number of programs that serve educators, community organizations, and students. Our website is eec4justice.com.

Introduction

In 2001, we began a journey of school reform to address the achievement gap. At the time we were working with a consortium of six school districts in the Metro East area of Illinois across the Mississippi River from St. Louis, Missouri. A long and insidious history of racism, corruption, and political strife has plagued this area for decades. These unfortunate distractions have victimized the local school districts. The effort to provide students with an effective learning opportunity regardless of the level of poverty, the constant presence of gangs and civil disorder, the precarious agenda of civic leaders, and overwhelming self-serving political initiatives have made reform difficult, bordering often upon the impossible. Our efforts toward reform would demand an approach that would be different from the countless other initiatives that the area had encountered with little or no results. We began this journey with a review of yet another educator who promoted reform in schools that became compelling, challenging, and in many respects, transformative.

John Dewey suggested that education is a process of living, and as such, is primarily a social institution (Dewey, 1990). This notion certainly strengthens an ideology that students participating in education ought to acquire the skills and knowledge to live as global citizens. Few would disagree that success in school is a precursor for success in life and that this expectation of school, lofty as it may appear, is realistic. Schools often ascribe to mission statements that profess the belief that all students can learn, and this focus in educational settings is to insure that happens.

Unlike Dewey's world of the early twentieth century, twenty-first-century challenges and possibilities include a world that has become increasingly small, where competition for jobs is global, where solving problems must be an exercise of heuristic thinking, and where advancements in technology outpace their application to everyday life. Include as well the efforts to attend appropriately to a classroom of diversity in which students reflect stark differences from those that Dewey's educators would have faced. Add yet one more complication for this "process of living," that of oppression and other forms of social injustices, which are endemic in the Metro East area as they are throughout this country.

Given Dewey's thoughts and the task upon which we were to embark, the notion of school as an agent for social justice advocacy became central to our efforts. Social justice can be a most illusive term as it is defined in numerous ways by individuals as well as institutions. For us, social justice advocacy, with a central focus upon racism for the Metro East area, cannot merely be an effort of description and debate. Instead it must be the formulation of policies and actions to respond to the injustices of those targeted by racism and any other form of oppression.

School leaders often see advocacy for issues of racism as a means to remediate unfairness within the school setting: unfairness as in issues of bullying, course selection, grade distribution, and/or advanced course opportunities. No one would doubt that these are important issues, but they tend to narrow the focus of racism upon a plan of remediation or restitution. Instead, our efforts were to prepare school leaders to address these issues in a much broader, comprehensive manner in which individual change is achievable and ultimately drives the needed systemic changes for reform.

Accomplishing this goal, we agreed, was a second-order change, i.e. rather than a focus upon the norms that create a status quo, our concern was with the conceptual framework upon which those norms rest. Thus, the deep change we were seeking was not merely cosmetic but instead substantive. With this in mind, we defined social justice advocacy:

Social justice advocacy is a critical consciousness that confronts policy, practice, and cultural nuance that prohibits certain students from successful learning opportunities and performance.

The inclusion of a "consciousness" provided us a platform upon which the affective domain of feelings, attitudes, dispositions, and assumptions could be addressed with the same rigor as the cognitive domain of analysis, causation, and application. Our reform effort quickly began shaping itself as a balance of "stance"—a very personal manner in which individuals see, feel, and interact with others, and "strategies"—the manner in which we essentially do our work, teach our children, and lead others. We recognized that this professional development, which would place racism as a major context for discussion, would be complicated, with issues of stance reflecting a range of emotions (confusion, anger, denial, resistance, struggle, and hurt). As it happens, during this same period, *Education Week* (August 8, 2001) published an editorial regarding racism and the achievement gap written by Julian Weissglass, in which he states:

> Any reform effort designed to reduce the achievement gap that does not help whites and people of color heal from the hurts of racism will not likely succeed over time. Although educator cannot, by themselves, solve all the problems caused by racism in society, it is possible for us to construct healing communities in which people can learn how to listen and give attention while other heal.

Our journey in this professional development therefore became, as suggested by Weissglass, one of healing and since this is not a familiar term used in reform efforts of public schools, it required of us to agree upon the following grounding assumptions regarding the oppression of racism:

Assumption #1. We believe that the feelings of blame, shame, and guilt are elements that have helped to sustained racism and any other form of oppression in America. Spending time focusing blame on individuals is futile and does little to dismantle the system. We believe that shame and guilt, though real feelings, provide little energy for transforming individual lives. Thus, our work is to create a safe environment for individuals to explore a new way of thinking about self. We accept that feelings of blame, shame, and guilt may emerge from the work; however, we remind individuals that none of these emotions will help to reconnect us to our inherent goodness.

Assumption #2. We believe that conscious learning emerges from places of dissonance. Our social environment is one in which we receive countless messages that shape our thinking about self and others. We cannot escape these messages that all too often distort truth. These messages eventually become embedded in our dispositions regarding our own sense of identity as well as others different from ourselves. One means by which we can escape these messages is to confront them, and confrontation, for many, takes us to a place of dissonance. Therefore, we accept that this work may often lead folks to an uncomfortable place in which their own beliefs may be challenged. We believe that this "journey" which we often use to describe our work is filled with this kind of circumstance, and we often suggest that people "lean into the discomfort" in order to stay on the journey.

Assumption #3. We believe that racism, like all other forms of oppression, is a system developed to insure a dominant group both power and privilege over a targeted group held in subjection. Race is a social construct having no biological basis. But institutionalized racism is a system built entirely upon the color of one's skin along with a belief that humans are *not* created as equals. Consequently, People of Color, considered not fully human, would need the control of the "great White father." Furthering the growth of institutionalized racism is a system of capitalism benchmarked by benefits achieved through a free labor market in a primarily agricultural economy. Thus racism, as other oppressions, is intentional and like that of building a house, it has an architecture, supporting and sustaining the power of a dominant group while holding others in subjection and as objects of targeting. For this reason, we use a variety of theoretical models for individuals to understand and recognize the institutionalized oppressions we wish to dismantle.

Assumption #4. We believe that our unconscious mind drives many of our decisions regarding human interaction. We believe that we all carry a set of assumptions about others, assumptions that we have come to regard as truth. We believe that our effort to create an intentional and courageous examination of those "hidden" assumptions allow us to impact students' lives in a more meaningful, authentic fashion. Research has clearly identified the impact of teacher expectations and students' performance. Therefore, we believe this work helps to unravel the unconscious assumptions that each of us hold regarding the intellectual capacity of our students, and as well, how we view what constitutes "acceptable" behavior.

Given this background, we began a program entitled the Leadership and Racism Program (LRP). We piloted the program for two years in the Metro East area schools. Following the pilot programs, LRP has been adopted by numerous districts in Missouri, Illinois, Virginia, Pennsylvania, Wisconsin, and in partnership with other agencies in California. For over a decade, the LRP program has worked with over 2000 school leaders and faculty members. This LRP program is designed with a two-day retreat and four additional full days of follow-up sessions. Participants in this program consist of a cohort of approximately twenty-five to thirty teachers and administrators from a school district. The retreat is centered upon the disposition of stance and includes a format for conversations of **heart** (the affective domain) and

head (the cognitive domain). The follow-up sessions, though not neglecting the personal journeys of participants, focus on issues of strategies or conversations which involve the **hand**. It was our assumption that a focus on the development of a critical consciousness regarding racism and any other oppression would ultimately lead to changes that would have a positive impact on student performance. These changes would be reflected in instructional patterns, school-wide procedures, and systemic processes.

Who Is This Book For?

The purpose of this book is to offer social justice leaders, be they principals, teacher leaders, or professional development providers, a template upon which critical conversations regarding racism and any other oppression can be achieved. All too often, the value of professional development in education relies predominantly upon the acquisition of a new "strategy," a lesson plan that can be easily applied to the classroom or a policy adopted at the school level. While we have no doubt that these elements are important and serve a purpose, we also believe that they are not enough to accomplish the deep change that we seek in this work. With this in mind, the central focus of this template is to engage participants in authentic and honest discourse regarding racism and other forms of oppression.

How Is This Book Organized?

Creating these conversations is the lesson plan of this book. We have learned and now share a number of ways in which this "courageous conversation" can be created, sustained, and continued. We also acknowledge that a major pedagogy through which these conversations are accomplished is that of reflection. Here again we invoked the thinking of John Dewey who also suggested that reflection is the manner in which we re-conceptualize our thinking, truly a second-order change.

The activities within these templates will require an environment that offers participants a sense of safety, free from assaults of fault, blame, or shame. For this reason, the templates will include a number of suggestions for "setting the stage," "encouraging participation," and "mediating" the difficulty that will likely be encountered in the struggle to make sense of these issues. We also provide school leaders with the voices of past participants as their authentic responses serve well to enhance future efforts in this professional development process.

Chapter 1: Before You Begin: This chapter will examine some critical elements to guide the reader through the book. It is important to be transparent regarding the thoughts and ideas that have been used in this book to create and sustain courageous conversations. We also highlight the interconnectedness of identities and the impact that this interconnectedness has upon examining oppression beyond the scope of any one oppression (Lorde, 1983). This chapter will also share practices that we have used to strengthen the engagement of participants.

Chapter 2: "Designing Conversations": This chapter will introduce the reader to a reform effort as a healing process. As demonstrated by the chapter title, it is the confluence of one's heart, head, and hands that leads to effective school reform. The chapter will outline a number of methods that support engagement and promote authenticity within the conversations.

Chapter 3: A Conversation of the Heart: In this chapter we will benchmark the professional development process we have used to impact the dispositions, attitudes, and personal stance of social justice advocates. We will use the cycle of socialization to guide the reader through a process to explore these notions in a safe, forthright manner. We will also include a number of research projects that have been conducted over the years that help us understand the manner in which our unconscious mind informs our behaviors more often than our conscious mind.

Chapter 4: A Conversation of the Head: In this chapter we will propose a number of activities that assist educators in the development of new "thinking" regarding oppression, specifically racism, and its architecture. The elements of dominance and targeting exist in all forms of oppression. To effectively serve as a social justice advocate it is essential to understand the manner in which any oppression is established and sustained. We will also share the manner in which these activities offer a transference and applicability with all other forms of oppression that may exist within school settings.

Chapter 5: A Conversation of the Hand: This chapter will help the reader to connect the notions explored through the lens of heart and head to instructional practice and strategies. This chapter will focus primarily upon ways to strengthen practice to promote different behaviors. Included in this chapter are worksheets that prompt educators to examine what they might stop, start, or continue in their work as social justice leaders. Using typical disciplinary patterns, instructional practices, and school-wide policies, this chapter will offer a myriad of activities that can be readily used to improve instruction, support inclusiveness, and strengthen student engagement.

Chapter 6: Allies: We Can't Do This Alone: This chapter will emphasize the critical need for the development of allies to do this work. It will include findings from the research done with school leaders over the past decade. Four attributes of an ally will be benchmarked in this chapter that provide a practical view of behaviors necessary to create alliances across the various identities that exist within school settings.

Chapter 7: Lessons Learned: This chapter will essentially be a narrative of the lessons learned regarding these courageous conversations. Shared earlier, we have viewed this as a journey. As such, our own individual and personal lessons through our own individual identity will be shared. This chapter will also include a more complete examination of the research previously referenced. Past participants' voices will also be highlighted in this final chapter.

Special Features

This book has been written from a practitioner view and voice. Several activities in this book include worksheets that can be easily adapted for any particular school leaders' audience. Chapters that speak directly to the development of a conversation of the heart, head, and hands are organized with a specific sequence which we have found to be most effective. Thus, activities are platformed in a manner that allows individuals to examine their thinking and feeling at a deeper level. Frequently, we will emphasize the need for a safe environment in which all individuals can share their feelings, attitudes, and dispositions. We will provide a number of ways in which this "safe environment" can be created and sustained through conversation that can be difficult. Finally, we offer a number of facilitation tips that will guide a social justice leader before, during, and after their own courageous conversations.

References

Dewey, J. (1990). *The school and society and the child and the curriculum.* Chicago: University of Chicago Press.

Lorde, A. (1983). There is no hierarchy of oppressions. *Bulletin: Homophobia and Education,* 14(3/4): 9.

Weissglass, J. (2001, Aug. 8). Racism and the achievement gap. *Education Week.*

Before You Begin

There is no hierarchy of oppression.

(Audre Lorde, 1983)

Audre Lorde was a champion for the rights of individuals. As such, she provides us a lens on oppression that should be considered before you begin this book. Lorde reminds us that everyone's identities are an intricate fabric of experiences that reflect their lives (Lorde, 1983). She is Black, a lesbian, a feminist, and a poet. To ask her to only think about the injustice she encounters resulting from just one of those realities minimizes an effort to create social justice for all. The color of our skin, our age, our religious belief, our sexual orientation, our body type, even our socio-economic status, play out opportunities for power and/or targeting. Addressing social justice issues by neglecting all of the identities we possess serves only to diminish the efforts toward a social consciousness of freedom from intolerance. Lorde helps us to recognize the interconnectedness of oppression.

Black and White men each share a position of power given the oppression of sexism. However, a Black man doesn't hold the same power position within the oppression of racism. Black and White women both experience targeting within the oppression of sexism. However, within the oppression of racism, Black women are targeted while White women are empowered. The idea of the interconnectivity of the different oppressions is a focus of this activity that we often use with school leaders engaged in these conversations.

The Fabric of Oppression

Begin the facilitation of this activity with school leaders listing the ways in which they see their own identities. Encourage each individual to respond with not only their own sense of identity, but additionally how the "world"

1

Worksheet 1.1 Fabric of Oppression

"Ism"	Sexism	Ageism	Classism	Hetero-Sexism	Lookism	Racism
Identity	Sex	Age	Socio-economic status	Sexual orientation	Physical appearance	Race
Dominant Greater access to goods, services, benefits, and social advantage						
Targeting Lesser access to goods, services, benefits, and social advantage						

might see them. This allows for individuals who may be bi-racial to acknowledge that the world may see them as "White" in some cases, while "Black" in other circumstances. Promote sharing first in small groups and then in the full group about the numerous ways in which we see one another. There may be individuals who hold an identity as private. Therefore, this conversation does not require everyone to speak. Following this conversation, pass out Worksheet 1.1 as well as placing it in front of the group.

There are a number of "isms" that could be placed upon this chart. The diversity of the school leaders present will often determine the specific "isms" that are identified for the worksheet/chart, i.e. ability (mental and physical), religion, gender, color/hue. The conversation should first identify the dominant players and targeted players of each of the "isms." The next step is to explore in the larger group the various ways in which members of each group are either targeted or have dominance. This is not a discussion of morality or individual behavior, but instead an examination of the manner in which a system distributes and provides access to goods, services, and social advantages. For example, an individual who is exceedingly poor has little access to financial benefits or services resulting from his/her economic reality. Again, this individual's worthiness or morality is not in question, but instead the manner in which his/her access has been limited. An individual who is gay may not be able to acknowledge his/her partner in the social settings of the workplace. Thus this individual must contend with a diminished opportunity of social advantage. A Muslim may encounter a number of ways that his/her religion, dress, or holidays are denied in the workplace compared to someone who is Christian. Filling this table out illuminates for many how oppression distributes power to some, while denying opportunities to others.

Transference

The conversations in this book are predominantly about racism (oppression based on skin color). The architecture upon which any oppression is designed and sustained remains the same regardless of the "ism" we wish to discuss. It is an architecture that creates an unequal distribution of power and also creates a distorted view of those who have been targeted. With this in mind, we have learned that the exercises, handouts, and worksheets used in this book will give school leaders insights as to how to confront other forms of oppression. The Table of Oppression, introduced in Chapter 4, is true for any oppression and transference to another remains a valid application. Much like a log jam, the opportunity to move but one log will often lead to the liberation of the other logs. Our experience has been that the courageous conversation explored in this book often enables school leaders to address other oppressions that exist within their school setting, i.e. sexism, heterosexism, lookism, ageism, etc.

For this reason, we encourage readers of this book to adapt discussions of the Table of Oppression, and other activities that will be explored in the following chapters, to include issues relevant to their particular circumstances. We have done so in Santa Barbara, California where the Latino/a students by and large comprise the disenfranchised, oppressed group. In that same area, the work also included students who were Cambodian, Vietnamese, or Hawaiian, who are often invisible because of the homogenized term of "Pacific Islanders." Colonization, similar to racism, is the terminology used to describe the oppression experienced by Native Americans and Mexicans. Schools in the Kansas City area reflect a large number of Mexican Americans who encounter targeting within the school system. In many school districts throughout the nation a growing number of gay/straight alliances for students have emerged and represent again another context in which the issues of oppression can be addressed. Understanding how oppression divides us is a first step toward social justice advocacy.

> . . . and so long as we are divided because of our particular identities we cannot join together in effective political action.
>
> Audre Lorde

No Experts

We do not propose that we are experts. Our experiences with this work may have offered a bit more understanding, but we continue to be learners on this journey. For this reason, we often say, "have not arrived yet, just agreed to go." With that in mind, we encourage the reader to be willing to explore, feel, confront, and challenge personally the same activities you will facilitate with your professional staff. Leadership above all else is the capacity to influence, and this book provides a template for that effort. School leaders who truly influence others to think differently about their own stance and instructional strategies become allies for their constituents. An ally is someone who remains aware with an authenticity and courage to challenge self as well as others. An ally is someone who examines experiences with a sharper sense of acuity and acts as an agent of change, confronting the oppressions which threaten our sense of humanness. Leaders that serve as allies are those who bring about the reform we seek. Improving schools begins with improving self. These conversations are about healing from oppressions that hurt all of us albeit in different ways.

Suspend Certainty

Parker Palmer in the *The Courage to Teach* calls out our obsession with "thinking the world apart" (Parker, 1989). He suggests that Western civilization is committed to thinking in polarities. We make sense of things through a lens that is black or white, true or false, right or wrong. In conversations, we often respond to opposing viewpoints with "but," suggesting that whatever might have been shared is negated and a different point of view must be accepted. We grip tightly that which we label as certain. In a way, our certainty provides a kind of safety zone. It becomes comfortable and allows us a point of view to which we attach our ego and ultimately our sense of self. We protect that certainty and give it a rationality that overshadows or denies confrontation. Peter Senge wrote about *metanoia*, a Greek word meaning a fundamental shift or change or, more literally, transcendence (Senge, 1990). In this work and these courageous conversations we ask people to suspend certainty. We ask that individuals allow a fundamental shift in thinking, i.e. a transcendence to occur. It's not the easiest thing to do, but in that suspension people often find a new way of thinking.

For example, when talking about racism, the concept of privilege is exceedingly hard for White men to grasp. For some White men, acknowledging privilege also means denying one's hard work and effort. Again, we hear in that thinking a polarity, one of this or that, true or false, right or wrong, *privilege or hard work*. Instead, when we ask individuals to suspend certainty, and consider that privilege and one's hard work can inhabit the same space, one participant exemplified that view by sharing: "I have worked hard *and* I've lived in a system that gave me privilege because of the dominant position in which I was born." We believe that the core of all humans is goodness, and we also accept that goodness does not excuse any of us from being clueless as to the ways in which oppression operates.

Our most conscious learning, the lessons in our life of greatest importance, usually arrives because of dissonance. Dissonance is to experience an event, feel an emotion, or view a circumstance that doesn't fit our thinking and initially causes confusion. As we look at the stars and their travels through the night, it appears that we are indeed at the center of our solar system. But Copernicus caused a great deal of dissonance when he suggested and proved that the Sun rather than the Earth was the center of the solar system. And now we can put men on the moon, and perhaps someday, people on Mars. Thinking differently and avoiding the comfort of certainty is a powerful way in which we resolve and heal from the oppressions that surround us. It is the path through which we are truly liberated.

No Blame, Shame, or Guilt

Throughout this book, you will hear often the reminder of no blame, shame, or guilt. Each of these emotions can cause silence, and silence is the best friend of any oppression. Thus, a major role of anyone facilitating these kinds of conversation is to work against the elements that would cause participants to go silent. We encourage individuals to listen with the idea that whoever may be speaking is sharing genuinely with good intent. We suggest that these emotions (blame, shame, and guilt) are the tools by which oppression stays in place. Blame has been of little use in changing a system. Instead it merely manifests as confrontation, denial, withdrawal, and, in its worse case, violence. Shame and guilt are emotions that are held inside oneself and will often cause inertia. These emotions do not provide impetus toward change.

In *Other people's children: cultural conflicts in the classroom*, Lisa Delpit explores the ways in which voices are silenced (Delpit, 1995). Take for instance these voices:

> One thing that I struggle with as an individual when it comes to discussions about race is the fact that I tend to give up. When I start to think: "he or she will never understand me. What is the point?" I have practically defeated myself.

Often I feel that because I am White, my feelings are disregarded or looked down upon in racial dialogues. I feel that my efforts are unappreciated. I also realize that it is these feelings which make me want to withdraw from the fight against racism altogether.

In our class discussion, when White students were speaking, we sounded so naïve and so "young" about what we were discussing. It was almost like we were struggling for the words to explain ourselves and were even speaking much slower than the students of color. For these students the feelings, attitudes, and terminology came so easily.

When I'm participating in a cross-racial dialogue, I prefer that the people I'm interacting with understand why I react the way that I do. When I say that I want understanding, it does not mean that I'm looking for sympathy, I merely want people to know why I'm angry and not be offended by it.

Each of these statements is genuine and provides a view of what might cause participants to withdraw from the conversation. Not surprisingly, when asked how often one's identity has been part of a normal family conversation, those who are in a targeted group respond often, while those in a dominant group respond seldom. Consequently, creating a safe place for this conversation must be carefully established. In Chapter 2 we offer a set of norms to assure that kind of safe environment. We remind people as well of the value of conversation and that, "Conversation is the natural way in which humans think together" (Wheatley, 2002, p. 29).

References

Delpit, L. (1995). *Other people's children: Cultural conflicts in the classroom.* New York: The New Press.

Lorde, A. (1983). There is no hierarchy of oppressions. *Bulletin: Homophobia and Education,* 14(3/4): 9.

Parker, P. (1989). *The courage to teach: Exploring the inner landscape of a teacher's life.* San Francisco: Jossey-Bass.

Senge, P.M. (1990). *The fifth discipline: The art and practice of the learning organization.* New York: Doubleday.

Wheatley, M. (2002). *Turning to one another: Simple conversations to restore hope to the future.* San Francisco: Berrett-Koehler Publishers, Inc.

2 | "Designing Conversations"

Human conversation is the most ancient and easiest way to cultivate the conditions for change—personal change, community and organizational change, planetary change.
(Margaret Wheatley, 2002)

We agree with Wheatley's position regarding conversation and its value as a way to cultivate change. We believe that conversations of reform are designed, as illustrated in the chapter title, from the confluence of our heart, head, and hands. We also believe that the kinds of conversations that lead to that cultivation are neither spontaneous nor accidental. Instead they emerge from the intentional design of social justice leaders that promotes reflection and provides direction. Within this chapter we will present five attributes of design that have proven to nurture engagement, participation, and continual reflections.

Conversations of head, heart, and hand requires a very personal exploration and so we often refer to this work as a courageous conversation. Involvement of the affective domain (our heart) as well as the cognitive domain (our head) ultimately determines what actions (our hands) we might take for dismantling oppressions. Another dimension of this exploration must also include how each of us, regardless of our identity, is hurt by oppressions. Healing therefore is an element of this reform effort. Julian Weissglass in his editorial for *Education Week* in 2001 states that healing from the oppression of racism is necessary for any initiative to address the achievement gap (Weissglass, 2001):

Any reform effort designed to reduce the achievement gap that does not help whites and people of color heal from the hurts of racism will not likely succeed over time. Although educators cannot, by themselves, solve all the problems caused by racism in society, it is possible for us to construct healing communities in which people can learn how to listen and give attention while others heal.

Attribute of Design: Balance

Weissglass's thoughts encourage school reform to be centered upon personal stance as well as strategic behavior. Clearly this places the affective domain, that slippery landscape of attitudes, dispositions, and feelings, on an equal footing with what we have in the past accorded to the cognitive domain of analysis, causation, and application. Thus, an attribute for design for this conversation is to find a proper balance between stance and strategies.

Using Worksheet 2.1 will exemplify that kind of balance. School leaders filling in this information will recall both cognitive and affective memories. The questions within this worksheet bring memories of both circumstances

Worksheet 2.1 First Encounter—Someone Different

Recall your first interaction (beyond being a casual "passerby") or event with someone of a different identity (race, gender, age, ethnicity, etc.)
When did this take place in your life?
What were the circumstances that caused this to happen?
What were your feelings regarding this experience?
What contradictions did you encounter?
What remains in your thinking about this event?

as well as feelings regarding this first encounter. The worksheet is also safe in the sense that it is not drawing any particular judgment or conclusion regarding this personal experience.

Exploring this singular life event will often bring to the surface a myriad of feelings from which further conversation can grow. Participants of these conversations will often say:

> I've never really thought about this event.
> I'm surprised by how old I was before this encounter.
> I'm wondering why I had this feeling of fear.
> I really had to rethink what I felt about someone different from me.
> I was really lucky to have lots of diversity in my life when I was really young.
> I was troubled by how different he was from what I thought he would be.

This simple exploration is not about shame or blame, thus the openness for conversation grows out of curiosity resulting from circumstance. For this reason, it becomes an invitation to explore deeper the "lens" through which we see or feel regarding the diversity we encounter in our lives.

Attribute of Design: Conditions for the Conversation

These kinds of conversation become very personal and do not lead to a tangible "lesson plan," so often the demand of professional development in education. Social justice leaders must therefore provide an environment which will be safe, honest, and accepting of whatever emotions that might emerge. For this reason, another attribute of design is the development of conditions for safety, honesty, and acceptance. In Margaret Wheatley's book she offers the following conditions, which we have found most useful (Wheatley, 2002).

- We acknowledge one another as equals.
- We try to stay curious about each other.
- We recognize that we need each other's help to become better listeners.
- We slow down so we have time to think and reflect.

- We remember that conversation is the natural way humans think together.

- We expect it to be messy at times.

Another set of conditions is introduced as an acronym of a tool of a life-guard, the floater tied to a rope that can be tossed to a swimmer challenged by the water. The conditions established by this acronym provide school participants the opportunity to be safe, respected, and heard as we struggle with the messy conversations of oppression.

R—O—P—E—S

Each of these letters are introduced with the following descriptions. After sharing each letter and corresponding description, we always offer participants the opportunity to add to the list if they so choose. In so doing, we are benchmarking Wheatley's point of **"we acknowledge one another as equals."**

R—respect and responsibility. Although these words seem to carry a common definition, it is still helpful to ask individuals to share how respect might look or feel for them. The variety of responses can often give everyone a broader view of respect. Further, asking others to share what would be responsible behavior is helpful in this conversation. This does not have to be a lengthy dialogue, but asking others what their thoughts might be regarding these terms is necessary to create a greater sense of ownership for these standards.

O—openness, oops, and ouch. If we have not been talking or even thinking about race and racism, the idea of being open in this conversation can be difficult and can lead some individuals to disengage from the conversation. For this reason, we offer oops and ouch as tools for achieving openness for this conversation. The use of oops and ouch becomes signals that may pause a conversation and result in greater understanding. Without any doubt, we have all made statements that, given the chance, we would have said differently. Those are the times we wished we could have said: "Oops, that came out poorly, let me take the words back and give this more thought." So, during this conversation we welcome "oops" and give folks that opportunity.

In a similar way, a participant might notice feelings or thoughts in response to another participant's words or behaviors that block active and ongoing engagement with the conversation. Someone's "oops" might have caused another's discomfort or pain. Saying "ouch" becomes another signal that might stop the process, so that we can hear what is causing pain or discomfort.

These tools are not to create a debate, or justify a feeling. Nor are the tools used to assign blame or shame. Instead they are ways for the conversation to grow **"in which people can learn how to listen and give attention while others heal"** (Weissglass, 2001).

P—participate, pass. Educators, at times, will arrive for professional development with a focus upon anticipation as in: What is next on the agenda? When is the break scheduled? How much time for lunch? For this reason, and as a contrast, we ask folks to think instead with a focus upon participation. Conversations of this nature must be free-flowing as much of this work is interactive and dialogue-based. The agenda, therefore, will not include a time period for each activity in order to ensure a fluid conversation. We also acknowledge, on some occasions, individuals may choose to pass. It may be that a feeling or thought is confusing and attempting to voice it may feel threatening. We do suggest humorously though that you only have one pass, so use it wisely.

E—expect positive intent, speak from your experience using an "I" voice, *escuchar.* Listening to others is particularly relevant in this work given the societal norm of "not talking about race." Again, when we are just learning to talk about race, we are often not clear about our own thoughts and feelings. We need time and attention to form our thoughts and describe our feelings. Each of these standards are offered to assist us in the conversation. Expecting positive intent from each participant avoids the trap of judging statements too quickly. Often we speak with the plural pronoun "we" as if all of one group holds a similar thought. Speaking in an "I" voice allows the thought to be singular and not collective to a group.

Finally the Spanish word *escuchar* means to listen. Great emphasis is placed on the importance of being able to really listen and hear those words that individuals are sharing. We will often share a euphemism that perhaps might come from a grandmother who said: "God gave you two ears and one mouth for a reason."

S—sense of humor, said here, stays here. Talking about race and racism is difficult, often filled with struggle, and at times an appropriate level of humor is not merely helpful, but essential. Humor can change the energy within the room. Humor can invite folks into the conversation. Laughter shared is yet another way of creating connections. Humor can release tension and when used appropriately serve well to keep a conversation going.

Confidentiality requires deliberate elaboration and attention. When folks are involved in listening pairs (described later in this chapter) it is important to respect that confidentiality. An individual in this process is free to share his/her own story, but not to share the story of their partners without first seeking permission in a timely manner. In doing this work, participants are encouraged to express their feelings, which should therefore receive the same degree of respect and confidentiality as any comments made by participants. Conversations of this nature can also include statements made within a particular context that if shared outside the professional development process can be easily misunderstood and cause difficulty for others. These elements assure a strong sense of safety as these conversations will likely surface vulnerability, confusion, frustration, and sadness.

Attribute of Design: Definitions

One of the ways to create an environment of engagement is the clarification of terms and definitions. For this reason early on, we make explicit the definitions used for this leadership development work. Our definitions originated with the National Conference of Community and Justice (NCCJ). This organization was founded in 1927 as the National Conference of Christians and Jews. It was in response to the anti-Catholic sentiment that was expressed in Al Smith's run for the Democratic nomination for the presidency. Over the years, the organization renamed itself as the Conference for Community and Justice and included issues of injustice of race, class, gender, and sexual orientation. The vision for this organization is to "make our nation a better place for all of us, not just some of us." The definitions that we have used for this work include:

- **Prejudice**: an attitude, opinion, or feeling formed without adequate prior knowledge, thought, or reason.
- **Discrimination**: the effective, injurious treatment of other groups so as to give an advantage to one's own group.
- **Oppression**: the one-way systemic mistreatment of a defined group of people, with that mistreatment reinforced and supported by society.
- **Racism**: a complex system of beliefs and behaviors, which are both conscious and unconscious, personal and institutional. They result in the oppression of People of Color and benefit the dominant group. It is a system grounded in the presumed superiority of the White race.

Worksheet 2.2 Definitions

Prejudice An attitude, opinion, or feeling formed without adequate prior knowledge, thought, or reason.	Prejudice is invisible; you really can't see a prejudice. You can make some assumption about what prejudice someone might harbor based upon their identity. But until they act, you don't really know. For this reason, a prejudice is much like a *tape* in one's head, one that was recorded as a result of childhood experiences, the circumstances of one's environment, and a myriad of messages received over the years about self and others. This tape can be conscious, but of equal consideration is the fact that it is also playing in an unconscious manner. Unconscious bias is not merely a notion, it is a fact.
Discrimination The effective, injurious treatment of other groups so as to give an advantage to one's own group.	Unlike a prejudice an *action* can be seen. Sometimes it is a very subtle action and seemingly innocent. Often the seemingly innocent discrimination emerges as a micro-aggression to those who have been targeted, i.e. "You are so articulate. Where are you from? You don't sound Black." In our work we do not measure an act of discrimination with regard to size, or excuse discrimination that may result from innocence. Instead we seek to understand discrimination at a personal level and of equal importance, at a level of policies and practices that covertly discriminate.
Oppression The one-way systemic mistreatment of a defined group of people, with that mistreatment reinforced and supported by society.	Oppression does not happen nor is it created and sustained by accident. Oppression is intentional, and is crafted with a particular *architecture* that holds it in place. Much like the construction of a building, there are structures that are designed to strengthen walls, hold weight, withstand outside pressures. Dismantling all forms of oppression must begin by understanding the manner in which it is built.
Racism A complex system of beliefs and behaviors, which are both conscious and unconscious, personal and institutional. They result in the oppression of People of Color and benefit the dominant group. It is a system grounded in the presumed superiority of the White race.	There are lots of words in this definition. Take a moment and share what words are compelling to you. Of course, we intend to examine this more fully as we work together. We are examining racism as one oppression in America. The oppression of racism is so delicately constructed in such an elegant manner that as Paolo Freire would suggest, it becomes a **"norm," a "status quo"** (Freire, 2004). It allows a default notion—"That's just the way the world is"—an illusion that we all have been tricked into thinking.

Certainly definitions of this nature can have numerous interpretations. There is no doubt that participants will bring their own perceptions of the validity of these definitions. In order for the conversations to move forward, rather than seeking agreement or even consensus regarding these definitions, we present them as the foundations for our work. We introduce the definitions for the purpose of transparency, a way of providing a "window" into our thinking. Worksheet 2.2 is used to introduce the definitions along with a dialogue for each.

Attribute of Design: Reflection as Pedagogy

Experience and reflection on experience are critical in the design for this courageous conversation. John Dewey believed that learning is both process and outcome (Dewey, 1990). It is not something done to us but, instead, emerges as we attempt to make meaning of what we have done ourselves. As you will see throughout this book, a number of activities are used for participants to share a common experience, something done together. Essential to this courageous conversation is, therefore, an intentional manner in which participants can reflect upon that common experience. Given the topic of racism, no doubt this conversation, in Wheatley's words, can easily get *messy*.

Quite often when conversations of racism get messy, we have a tendency to immediately impose conditions for civility and order. Conversations are scuttled when emotions of fear and anger become "loud" and "out of control." A reminder of the conditions as established at the beginning of the conversation can help return to a sense of reasonableness. Consequently, the following notions should be offered before entering into reflections that may also help the conversation from being scuttled. Consider the following:

- **"Lean into discomfort."** Activities suggested in this book can often cause participants to feel uncomfortable. We also know reflections can take any of us to a place of dissonance. Encouraging people to "lean" into the dissonance holds the promise of profound learning. We are asking people to move toward rather than away from complexity.

- **"Both/and."** The predominant model for which we have viewed professional knowledge emerges from nineteenth-century technical rationality. In this model empirical science is the only source of knowledge. Thus, our world is usually overwhelmed with an "either/or" disposition. Offering participants the opportunity to think in "both/and" terms opens the door for more possibilities, alternatives, and options.

- **"Feelings are as natural as breathing."** Many feelings will surface in these courageous conversations. We all have been socialized in multiple ways to deal with emotions. Emotions can often be viewed as embarrassing, uncontrollable, unrealistic, etc. Thus, giving permission for whatever feelings participants might encounter as a natural part of a process of reflection is helpful.

Reflection upon practice, as Donald Schon suggested, can be viewed as a swamp. The swamp is full of indeterminate zones of practice, ones that include uncertainty, uniqueness, and are dominated by values. It is in the swamp that we find problems of greatest human concern, and of course, racism is one of those of "greatest human concern" (Schon, 1987). Asking people to explore their own racial consciousness should not be threatened by imposing judgments of rightness, absolutes, and/or correctness. Worksheets that ask leaders to reflect upon personal stance should be constructed as a continuum rather than merely selecting a predetermined position.

An excellent example of this type of worksheet for reflection is created from the work of Gloria Ladson-Billings. In her book, *The Dreamkeepers: Successful Teachers of African American Children*, she draws a distinction between a culturally relevant teacher and an assimilationist teacher. Her work would define assimilationist teaching as a style that operates without regard to the students' particular cultural characteristics. In this style a teacher's role is to ensure that students fit into society which ultimately emerges from the stance of the teacher and how she/he sees the student. Thus a teacher with low expectations of a student will translate as that student fitting a lower rung of society.

In contrast, a culturally relevant teacher becomes the antithesis of the assimilationist teacher. A culturally relevant teacher is working from an understanding and an appreciation of a student's cultural background and not letting that identity limit a student's possible success. A culturally relevant teacher aims for excellence without an imposed limitation (Ladson-Billings, 1994).

Ladson-Billings's work examines eight teachers who have demonstrated significant success in teaching African American children. She provides a series of descriptions of assimilationist teaching and culturally relevant teaching. These descriptions include the following areas: conceptions of self and others, social relations, and conception of knowledge. Using her descriptions, ask each school leader to identify which of the characteristics best describe their own pedagogy. This is not a matter of judgment but instead a personal exercise in reflection upon practice. A worksheet of this nature, with a self-disclosure of opinion and supporting evidence, can offer participants a broad and comprehensive lens upon personal instructional practices.

Attribute of Design: Space

Paying attention to the space in which this conversation will take place may seem of little importance. Yet it has been our experience that attending to a few details regarding this space and how it is set up is an important design element. Meaningful conversation in which each participant's voice is both sought and valued is seldom accomplished in a corporate room with tables and chairs. The nature of that kind of room and the manner in which it is arranged will often establish a hierarchy such as the "head" of the table, chairs being different (some plush, others simple), name plates, and technology arranged for an obvious speaker and audience. Of course, these rooms serve important purposes, but for this courageous conversation, they do not engender the kind of open, honest, reflective conversation we are seeking.

Large rooms with lots of wall space, comfortable chairs without tables, and in a place other than the work setting is highly recommended. Off campus, at least for some individuals, will offer a bit of safety and may indeed encourage participation. Name tags, with only first names and no titles, are suggested. In addition, we ask for chairs that can easily be arranged in small group and large group configurations.

Circles are the preferred chair arrangement to begin the conversation. The circle symbol meaning is universal, sacred, and divine. It represents the infinite nature of energy, and the inclusivity of the universe. It also suggests equality, as every chair within the circle is both a beginning and an ending point. Circles are also a configuration in which everyone can see each other. Participants being able to see each other as reflections are shared, though subtle, offer a message of interest, curiosity, and inclusivity.

The space for this conversation must also have an assurance of privacy, another reason for seeking a place off campus. With little doubt, participants will share reflections that are meant only for those in the room. At times there will be emotions that are shared as participants encounter internal dissonance. It is important to protect this space from folks that may accidentally enter the space.

Some of the activities of these conversations involve flip chart papers that are displayed for participants to observe. Consequently, plenty of wall space is advisable. Music is also recommended. During reflection time, when participants may be writing in journals, soft music in the background sets a welcome ambiance for this important work. Once again, all these arrangements may seem obvious, but the more the room is arranged in this manner, the more participants will recognize the intentionality of this conversation.

The next three chapters will provide a template for facilitating these important conversations of the heart, head, and hands. As you explore this work, and begin to contemplate how these ideas may be adapted and infused into your own efforts for reform, we remind you that few of us are experts regarding this subject. Grappling with the manner in which we have all been socialized to play a part in oppressions no doubt suggests that we are all on a journey. As we often say; **"have not arrived yet, just agreed to go."**

References

Dewey J. (1990). *The school and society and the child and the curriculum.* Chicago: University of Chicago Press.

Freire, P. (2004). *Pedagogy of the oppressed.* New York and London: Continuum.

Ladson-Billings, G. (1994). *The Dreamkeepers: Successful teachers of African American children.* San Francisco: Jossey-Bass.

Schon, D.A. (1987, April). Education: the reflective practitioner. Paper presented at the annual meeting of the American Education Research Association, Washington, DC.

Weissglass, J. (2001, Aug. 8). Racism and the achievement gap. *Education Week.*

Wheatley, M. (2002). *Turning to one another: Simple conversations to restore hope to the future.* San Francisco: Berrett-Koehler Publishers, Inc.

3 | A Conversation of the Heart

Dr. Derald Wing Sue, a member of the Clinton Race Advisory Board, suggested that to achieve the task of creating the cultural mosaic of one America it would require addressing two difficult and unpleasant tasks: "a) an honest examination of unpleasant racial realities like racial prejudice, racial stereotyping, and racial discrimination and b) accepting responsibility for changing ourselves, our institutions, and our society." He went on to say that racism can no longer be viewed as "an intellectual concept for objective study" and "for the other person" but must be a conversation at a personal level of stance.

Entering the Conversation

As examined in Chapter 1, preparations for this conversation need to include all the suggested design elements. For a conversation of the heart, social justice leaders must also be able to feel safe and open. With that in mind, two activities help set the stage for the sharing of personal stories to build a sense of community among participants. As school leaders enter, have them create a poster with flip chart paper by answering the following questions and then placing the flip charts on the walls. (Facilitators should do the same and have them on the walls prior to the participants arriving.)

Name I prefer to be called:

1. I learn best when . . .
2. My current job is . . .

3. One of my favorite books is . . .

4. One person (alive or dead) that I would like to have lunch with is . . .

5. I identify as . . .

6. When I think of oppression I think . . .

7. When I think of racism I think . . .

These flip chart posters serve a dual purpose. First, by viewing others' posters each leader becomes a bit more familiar with members of this group beyond their names. Some commonalities are bound to be recognized among the participants. The posters serve as a way in which we become curious about one another: "**We try to stay curious about each other**" (Wheatley, 2002). A second purpose for this initial activity is for the facilitators to assess the makeup of the folks in the room, e.g. number of administrators, teachers, and/or other job titles, racial and gender balance, initial thoughts concerning oppression and racism.

Of greatest interest for the facilitator is question number five: "I identity as . . ." Many people struggle with that question and answers vary from: wife, husband, male, female, Christian, mother, father, etc. Identifying one's race as a response to this question is often and, seemingly, most easily done by People of Color. As participants in the cohort grow more comfortable and trusting of one another, this interesting pattern can be discussed again and will often lead to meaningful conversations about how and why disclosing racial identity is rarely considered as an identifier for some Whites.

Following this casual time of completing and viewing others' posters, the next step is to have everyone return to chairs arranged in a circle. Once seated, ask individuals to share by answering the following three questions:

What is your name?

What is your professional responsibility in this district?

What gift do you bring to any gathering?

The last question might present a bit of struggle for some. Once again, facilitators must also take the first risk by sharing the gift they bring to the gathering. This question does produce a positive energy within the room. Consequently the facilitator has more information regarding participants which will benefit the continual conversations. Humor, honesty, good listening skills, enjoyment of confrontation, seeking order, peacefulness— these are all various attributes of participating school leaders. Knowing these attributes gives a facilitator insight as to how some participants may react to probes and activities. If needed, this also gives the facilitator the chance to promote the importance of each person's voice and benchmarks yet another of Wheatley's condition: **"We recognize that we need each other's help to become better listeners."**

The second activity is to have individuals return to the posters and conduct a sticky note exploration. The poster that each participant made and displayed could be viewed as a kind of Table of Contents of their life. No doubt for each of the responses to the seven questions, there is likely a story, point of view, life experience to be shared. With this in mind, distribute packets of sticky notes. Instruct participants to use the sticky notes to ask questions, seek clarity, or respond to each other as they revisit all of the posters. The sticky notes are put directly on the posters and there is no need for names. Music in the background creates a pleasant atmosphere for this activity. Allow enough time so that each poster has two or three sticky notes. Before returning to the circle tell everyone to visit their own poster and pick a sticky note, choosing one that they feel comfortable sharing an answer or story probed by the note. In the large circle give each individual time to share their response to their chosen sticky note.

Many years ago Rabbi Nachman observed: "God so loved stories that he created man." These activities can help to develop a sense of community through the sharing of stories. The philosopher Paul Ricouer once observed: "Our own existence cannot be separated from the account we can give of ourselves. It is in telling our own stories that we give ourselves an identity" (Valdes, 1991).

In his book, *The Healing Wisdom of Africa*, Malidoma Patrice Some provides another reflection upon these initial activities. He uses the following narrative to describe the development of a community:

> What is required for the maintenance and growth of a community is not corporate altruism or a government program, but a village-like atmosphere that allows people to drop their masks. A sense of community grows where behavior is based on trust and where no one

has to hide anything. There are certain human powers that cannot be unleashed without such a supportive atmosphere.

The attention of the entire village to one person is motivated by the conviction that each person is the carrier of something that the village desires. The proof of this is in the fact of birth itself. A person's coming into the world testifies to the fact that one is a giver. And so everyone's behavior toward everyone else is based on the encouragement to develop each person's gift.

(Some, 1998, pp. 95–96)

It is fair to assume that participants will not necessarily enter this initiative recognizing the very personal "lens" which will be used throughout these conversations. Nor will they automatically connect this personal work with instructional practices or school policy. For this reason, it is advisable that another precursor for school leaders is a clear rationale from the district administration. School district mission statements frequently speak to issues of equity. These statements or strategic goals frame the focus of this professional development as exemplified by this example from one school district regarding their strategic focus: Provide curriculum and instructional approaches that prepare students for an increasingly diverse and global society.

The following are voices speaking to the positive impact of these opening activities:

- The safe environment to learn and process with peers and problem-solve.
- Hearing the experiences of others in the cohort and feeling their support.
- Sharing at the beginning of the day with other cohort members.
- Just listening to the journey some of us are on.

Listening Pairs

There is no doubt that a major attribute to a conversation of this nature is the critical need for individuals to truly listen to each other. We spend much of our time in "duologue," best described as a conversation where frequently the listener is thinking about what he or she might say back when the other person finishes talking. In these circumstances, our mind may only be constructing a response when it is our turn to listen. We are therefore distracted from listening by our desire to bring our own voice into a conversation to agree, disagree, seek clarity, express difference, or any of a number of other reasons.

For a conversation of the heart, listening as a duologue will not move participants to a deeper level of reflection. The willingness to hear a person's message, thoughts, insights, or story simply by being attentive to the words being shared is a truly valuable gift. The listening pair is an effective tool for conversations and it has its own process.

In the process, individuals are asked to listen to each other in a "knee-to-knee" or "side-by-side" dyad configuration. While in this configuration ask partners to choose who will go first, who will go second. Explain that while one partner speaks the other must only listen. The listener is instructed to not ask questions, seek clarity, or add their own voice during their partner's time for speaking. One analogy used to help the listener is for him/her to be "as a hollow reed through which the individual who is sharing can play his or her music." The speaker can then say whatever those first thoughts may be without being judged. Before beginning, share that each participant will have two minutes to respond to a particular probe.

The listening pair has the potential to establish a venue through which thoughts and feelings can be safely shared. The efficacy of the listening pair results from a listening partner who keeps his/her attention solely upon the person who is speaking. This undivided attention allows the speaker to express openly and feelings may surface during this time. We frequently suggest that feelings are not an accurate barometer of our thinking, however, until and unless we are able to address those feelings in a safe haven, we cannot get to our brilliant thinking.

To listen to another person with this level of sensitivity and non-judgmental attitude can change the emotional landscape of the speaker. What often happens is that the individual is able to reach deeply within, express feelings while simultaneously processing the origins, circumstances, and experiences that created those feelings. The listening pair allows participants to surface the kinds of feelings which are often connected to a personal racial consciousness. Participants who are given this opportunity to address irrational and stereotypical assumptions regarding race or any other identity without blame, shame, or guilt are more empowered and willing to adopt new thinking. Dr. John Gray suggested in *Men are from Mars, Women are from Venus* that: "What we can feel, we can heal" (Gray, 1997).

Worksheet 3.1 Listening Pair Process and Reflections

Participant responses	Process questions	Facilitator's reflection
"It was really hard to talk about myself."	Why is it so hard for you to speak well about yourself? What gets in your way of sharing positive thoughts about yourself with another individual?	We have been socialized to think that if we share positive comments about ourselves, we are bragging. That is not the case and in facilitating this exercise emphasis is placed on the use of the word **validating** as opposed to the use of the word bragging.
"It was really hard to stay quiet. I wanted to enter the conversation."	Understandable; describe your feelings when you had the undivided attention of the person who was listening to you.	The focus of this process of listening is on what we often call "listening with *the inner ear.*" Participants in the dyad who are operating in the roles of listener should strive to establish an invitational space for the speakers to "say" or "feel" whatever is surfacing. The sole objective of the listener is to do just that—listen, while simultaneously beaming delighted attention toward the person speaking.
"It was difficult to keep my mind focused only on listening."	That's not unusual! What do you think gets in our way of really being able to listen deeply to another person?	We understand how hard it is to simply sit and listen. In this world of multitasking and frenetic energy being the "normal" state of modus operandi, when we are faced with the simplicity of an exercise that only requires us to listen, it feels odd. With practice, this quiet but not passive state of giving attention to another person can be extremely effective in helping a person reach inward.
"I was feeling really good about listening to her talk about herself in that positive manner."	What were the feelings that came up for you as you listened? What feelings do you think surfaced for your partner when listening to you?	When comments like these are made it is such a powerful confirmation of how our thoughts can influence our feelings.
"I was surprised by how much we had in common though we have never met."	Why do you think you were able to connect so deeply with your listening partner and only in the span of two minutes?	The efficacy of this "hollow reed" listening is clearly made manifest when individuals are able to transcend and connect above and beyond differences.

Many educators have been schooled regarding active listening in which the behavior of the listener is to promote feedback, seek clarification, and offer paraphrasing to assure understanding. Clearly the listening pair requires a very different approach and as such does require practice. The following is an example of how to begin the practice with these directions. Worksheet 3.1 shares participants' responses with suggested processing questions and facilitator reflections.

Directions

Share with your partner all the good things about yourself. You may not use conditional terms such as "I think . . ." or "maybe." You must use robust adjectives concerning your goodness, such as "I'm the best . . ." or "No one is as good as me . . ." If you run out of things to share, repeat what you have said. Don't worry about time, we will keep track of that and let you know when to switch partners. Remember if you are the listener, your role is to listen only. (Time: two minutes.)

Listening pairs serve as well in other circumstances. First, finding words that bring meaning to a past experience in a safe space without being judged is a gift to everyone. Second, the listening pair is also useful as a tool to change the energy in the room. Conversations of the heart can at times create confusion, disagreement, resistance, and withdrawal. Forming a listening pair in those moments with the probes such as: "What is coming up for you?," "What are you feeling?," What is difficult for you right now?" can re-engage participants toward a path of understanding and empathy.

Cycle of Socialization

A song from the musical *South Pacific* about hate entitled "You've Got to Be Carefully Taught," states a poignant truth. We don't enter the world with a set of dispositions toward differences. How we see and feel about difference is not an accident, but instead a process of learning. Racial identity, our own and others, is developmental. It is quite evident that it is "carefully taught." Thus following the establishment of the conditions for conversations, a common set of definitions (as described in Chapter 2), and the tool of listening pairs, the next step in this conversation of the heart begins with the exploration of the cycle of socialization.

In the late 1980s, research suggested that an individual's personality development results from both interior and exterior realities. Lawrence Kohlberg, in his work regarding stages of moral development, offered the idea that there were distinct experiences—pre-conventional, conventional, and post-conventional—which lead to a set of abstract ethical principles upon which individual's live their lives (Kohlberg, 1984). Eric Erickson provided a set of eight stages by which individuals construct meaning and understanding (Erickson, Paul and Gardner, 1959). Additionally, George Mead developed a theory of social behaviorism upon which social experiences develops an individual's personality (Mead, 1913). Thus, a "cycle" of experiences and circumstances begins to socialize us and constructs a consciousness regarding differences. Exploring this cycle is particularly worthy in this conversation of the heart. The following narrative is used as a first step prior to introducing the cycle of socialization.

I would guess that many or you at some point in your life have been in the presence of a newborn baby. What is it that you see as you observe this newborn baby boy or girl? *(Solicit responses)*

If you happen to observe the newborn in a nursery, you probably see the little boys in blue blankets, and the little girls in pink blankets. The socialization starts immediately at birth. It has already begun to suggest colors as links to gender. As parents or caring adults we purchase clothes that contribute to a socialization of children. We may buy a shirt for the boy that says "Little Slugger" and one for the girl that says "Ballerina." Consider the types of toys that are identified for boys and girls. How about even ideas of dealing with difficulties in which we might say: "Big boys don't cry." *(Solicit responses)*

Let's fast forward; this little baby crawls into this room and enters our circle. The baby looks around and sees all these "big" people. The baby crawls over to one person and plays with this person until the person is tired. The baby crawls over to the second person and plays with this person until this person is tired. Eventually, the baby makes his or her way around the circle until everyone has had an opportunity to play with the baby. At no time did the baby enter the circle and decide where to go or who to go to based upon race, gender, religion, sexual orientation, class, and/or the way one looks. The baby just saw an opportunity to be loved, to be played with, to be hugged, to be fed, to be cuddled, to be cared for, and to be nurtured.

However, at some point on this baby's journey in life, the baby receives messages about differences. Somewhere along life's journey for this young person, messages were received that led to decisions regarding safety, health, morality, and a host of other attributes that became associated with differences. Those messages would suggest that if you "were different from me based on what I have been taught or told, then something is wrong with you." Sadly, it is not our differences that separate us, it is our inability to accept, recognize, embrace, and celebrate our differences.

We get these messages from all aspects of life—family, friends, faith-based communities, media, and of course school. *(Talk with a partner, about what you learned in history about people different from you.)*

Worksheet 3.2 Cycle of Socialization

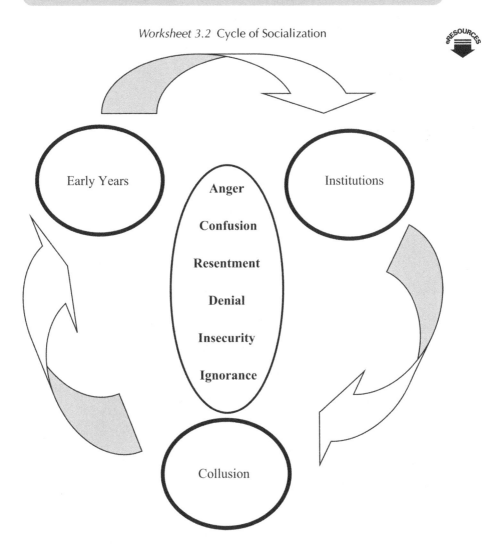

The model of the cycle of socialization shown on Worksheet 3.2 is adapted from Dr. Roberta Harro's work which appeared in Hardiman and Jackson's 'Conceptual foundations for social justice courses' (1997). It is comprised of three circles representing the manner in which the outside world has influenced the way we think about others and ourselves. Using this model in a PowerPoint presentation and letting each of the three circles appear one at a time allows time for clarification and discussion of each circle in the cycle of socialization.

First Circle: The Early Years

We all enter a world without blame, shame, guilt, or choice. No one selected their parents or the circumstances of their birth. However, we are born into

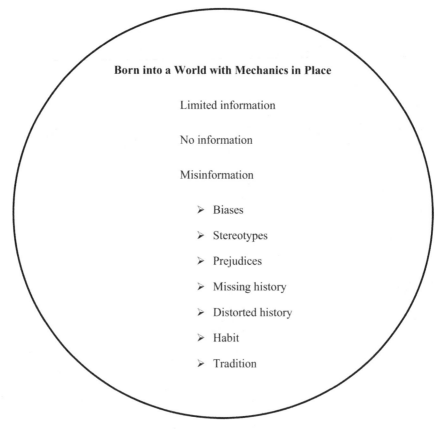

Figure 3.1 Cycle of Socialization: Installation

a world where mechanics are in place, which included biases, stereotypes, prejudices, missing history, distorted history, habit, and tradition. This is analogous to the visual of our definition of prejudice, a "tape," conscious and unconscious, which impacts our thinking about ourselves and those different from ourselves. Often these messages come from loved ones and significant persons in our lives. They come to us as well from the media, our faith-based affiliations, and of course school. Messages of this nature enter our consciousness in a variety of ways. Some are positive and offer to each of us a sense of belonging, acceptance, and love, and enrich our sense of the value of differences.

Other messages carry a very different context that would suggest fear, danger, hate, avoidance, and diminish our sense of humanity. Some are clearly spoken messages: "All Jewish people are rich," "White people can't be trusted," "People of Color are mean or dangerous." Others are subtle behaviors: a mother might hold her child's hand tighter as she encounters a man of color, or children in the back seat of a car are told to lock their doors while driving through a particular neighborhood. All these messages begin to shape our thinking about ourselves and others.

Messages that we received early on in history classes in school are often distorted or correct information is missing. Women are seldom portrayed in positions of prominence, influence, or leadership in the early development of our country. Genocide of indigenous people by Columbus and other European explorers is seldom discussed but, instead, many explorers are benchmarked as liberators. Slavery in our history books, a hideous narrative of our country, is often sanitized with condescending pictures of "happy slaves" or stories of the "Good Plantation Owners." In 2010, the Texas State Board of Education attempted to rewrite history in the state books with the following recommendations:

- The Slave Trade would be renamed the Atlantic Triangular Trade.
- Civil Rights would be described as "unrealistic expectations of equal outcomes."
- Enslaved people would be renamed as "unpaid interns."

Fortunately these recommendations were never adopted, but it does exemplify how the history we choose to tell becomes a major player in the socialization process.

Peter Taubman's work regarding identity development calls this early stage the creation of a "fictional register" filled with distortion and serving to imprison us as subjects leading to alienation and objectification (Taubman, 1993). Form small groups of three to four participants across race and gender, and use the following probes for individuals to share their stories. Following this small-group conversation, bring participants back to a large group to continue the discussion.

- How do the toys and clothes that we buy for our young children impact their sense of self?
- What kinds of messages do we send regarding discipline for boys and girls?
- What behavior expectations do we place on young boys and girls?
- What did you learn in school in your early years about women, men, members of a different race or culture?
- What were the images of heroes or villains you received as a young child from television, movies, or books?

Second Circle: Institutions

This second stage in the cycle is that of formal institutions and culture that either reinforces or refutes these earlier messages. Institutions like these we encounter every day. They are ubiquitous and we are bombarded with their

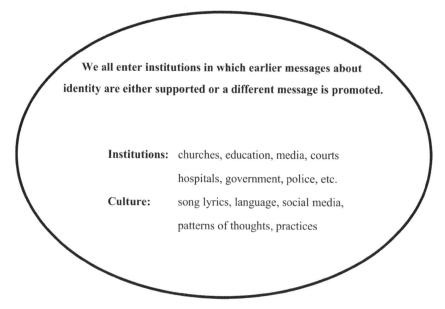

Figure 3.2 Cycle of Socialization: Internalization

messages continuously. This would include the media, government, houses of worship, economics, and again, education. Of course, there will be those who would suggest that each of these institutions also provides positive messages regarding identity. We certainly acknowledge and accept that truth. However, the frequency of messages of inclusiveness, acceptance, and appreciation fall short of those messages that serve to divide, question, and devalue differences.

These messages, as in the early years, become a part of our conscious and unconscious thinking. They often create a kind of "either/or" disposition that results from a particular ideology, posture, or political disposition. All of these dispositions influence our ideas regarding policies and practice. Each of these institutions also includes a lens through which objectives are accomplished, strategies are agreed upon, and evaluative processes are adopted. These lenses are also impacted by bias, discrimination, and injustice.

Follow the approach shared earlier, use the following probes in the small-group settings and subsequently in the large group to explore this circle of the cycle:

- What are the racial identities of people in the top government positions?
- How do our health care institutions reflect bias or discrimination?
- What does Sunday morning look like regarding diversity, inclusiveness, and acceptance?
- How do our laws and penal systems reflect racial neutrality?
- What role and to what degree does the media impact the reinforcement of messages of your early years?
- What are the history lessons that we all learned regarding the formation of our country?
- What are the subtle words in literature, media, and social networks that reinforce stereotypes?

Third Circle: Collusion

Without some form of interruption of the negative messages received in our early years and reinforced by institutions, feelings that may emerge in individuals include anger, confusion, resentment, denial, insecurity, and stress. Emotions of this nature lead to violence, crime, horizontal violence,

Figure 3.3 Cycle of Socialization: Collusion

inconsistency, and internalization of patterns of power, as well as internalization of diminished self-worth. For these reasons we refer to this circle as one of collusion and, further, we also suggest that passing on these negative messages can be both a conscious and unconscious act.

In *The Tipping Point*, Malcom Gladwell explores the unconscious messages we carry regarding stereotype and bias using the Implicit Association Test (Gladwell, 2000). The Implicit Association Test was first developed in 1998 and has been extensively used to measure how implicit attitudes (*tapes*) mediate favorable or unfavorable feelings, thoughts, or actions within social settings. Referencing this work helps the facilitator to again highlight how our stance, that is our feelings, thoughts, dispositions, and attitudes, ultimately impacts our behaviors and emerges from both our conscious and unconscious thinking.

In *The Hidden Brain*, Shankar Vedantam examines rigorous scientific studies and experimental evidence to explain the impact the unconscious mind has upon behaviors. One of those research projects involved placing certain pictures above a coffee pot in an office hallway with a honor system for payment. During the weeks that the picture of flowers was on the coffee pot, the money collected fell far short of the cost. The weeks that a flower picture was replaced with the picture of eyes, the money collected exceeded cost. Though the office workers did not remember the pictures, their behavior was altered in measureable ways. The researchers' conclusions were that our unconscious mind observes everything, even what might be in the peripheral (Vedantam, 2010).

For this reason, a final conversation, initially in small groups, and then in the larger circle, is a method to examine the ways in which we all consciously and unconsciously collude with the negative messages of the cycle.

- What are the ways in which we unconsciously promote the status quo?
- What might be the difficulty for change, for raising consciousness, for interrupting?
- How do we begin to take a stand or question?
- How do we begin to reframe our own racial consciousness?
- How does our language collude with stereotypical messages?
- What stories do we share with our children regarding social interactions?
- How do we unconsciously create either acceptance or rejection?

Things I Heard and Learned

A final activity in this conversation which explores the impact of the cycle of socialization on a very personal level is "Things I Heard and Learned." Worksheet 3.3 offers participants the time to recall those early messages from family and friends, the media, faith-based affiliations, and school. Prior to distributing this worksheet, the following directions should be given: Recall the messages you might have heard from these four areas regarding the identity groups listed on the worksheet. Try to recall the message without censoring the statements. Try to recall the messages that you might have heard between the ages of eight through fifteen (a significant age in which individual identity is being developed).

It is also important to emphasize with participants that they are not at fault for the messages recalled. Likely some people will recall statements that are hurtful, biased, and may be embarrassing to write on the work-sheet. Remind individuals that these are messages that they did not seek and resulted from circumstances for which they had no control. Stating the exact words and noticing the feelings those words evoke is part of the process. These are not messages that they believe, but instead merely what was heard and learned early in life.

This worksheet is an example of ones that have been used with our past school leaders. The table can be amended for whichever identity groups are involved in this conversation, e.g. Christians, Muslims, Jews, etc.

Worksheet 3.3 Things I Heard and Learned

Groups	Family/Friend	Media	Faith-based	School
Indian Native American				
African Black American				
European White American				
Women				
GLBTQ				
Hispanic Latino/a				
Asian/Pacific Islander				
Circumstance of Poverty				
Circumstance of Disability				

After a reasonable amount of time for individuals to fill out the worksheet, small groups should be formed to further discuss this activity. Facilitators should create groups with diversity in mind. Sharing in small groups allows folks to recognize commonalities. Often individuals will have similar experiences that result from living in a rather homogeneous setting. Not surprisingly, participants will share what their early years were like living in a "bubble" where everyone was of similar identity, background, faith etc. Groups with a variety of ages will encounter different words that convey a similar message regarding a particular identity. During this time of sharing, there is often laughter as participants recall how "silly" a message might have sounded.

As groups explore this information collectively, facilitation probes should include:

- Which of the columns (family/friends, media, faith, school) seemed to be easiest to recall?
- What kind of feeling did you have during this activity?
- What did you notice in your group conversation that surprised you?
- Did you have any blank spaces?

The last question regarding blank spaces has become an important reference point. Blank spaces carry a kind of message as well, one of invisibility, unimportance, or of little value. As explained earlier, the Implicit Association Test (IAT) suggests that perhaps there are no blank spaces. Our unconscious mind operates from both explicit and implicit messages. As the flowers or the eyes on the coffee pot created a behavior response so, too, will messages that may hide in our unconscious mind.

Exploring the messages one heard as a child is a first step toward a path of liberation. As stated earlier, some of these messages may still live in our unconscious minds. Discovering what may still exist in our unconscious mind is a first step in interrupting old thought patterns and creating new ones in support of a path of liberation, no doubt a courageous exploration but one that is an essential element for social justice leadership.

> More and more, I have gotten to think that some part of our brain is still stuck where we were at four and five and eight and it is always there. Under stress, people do regress to an early mode.
>
> (Frances Aboud, 2003)

Continuing Reflections

Often, anti-racist efforts describe what others do to each other. Race is used to discriminate or empower individuals and groups. Action is generally a leader's efforts to remediate the unfairness that racial tension and animus have created. Of course, this is a legitimate task for social justice leaders and will likely result in plans of remediation or restitution. No one would doubt that reacting to the injustices of racism and all forms of oppression is the mission of social justice leadership.

The choice of interrupting or confronting the manner in which the cycle of socialization has created a personal stance ought to be a continuing conversation. Frequently leaders who revisit this activity uncover other dispositions that had not surfaced previously. The effort of these activities is proactive rather than reactive and thus offers individuals a sense of liberation, empowerment, and control without the need for blaming, shaming, or a feeling of guilt. It is the very nature of the healing suggested earlier (Weissglass, 2001).

References

Aboud, F. (2003). the formation of in-group favoritism and out-group prejudice in young children: Are they distinct attitudes? *Developmental Psychology*, 39(1): 48–60.

Erickson, E.H. Paul, I.H. and Gardner, R.W. (1959). *Psychological issues* (Vol. 1). Madison, CT: International University Press.

Gladwell, M. (2000). *The tipping point.* Boston: Little, Brown and Co.

Gray, J. (1997). *Men are from Mars, Women are from Venus.* New York: HarperCollins.

Hardiman, R. and Jackson, B.W. (1997). Conceptual foundations for social justice courses. In M. Adams and L.A. Griffin (Eds.), *Teaching for diversity and social justice: A sourcebook.* New York: Routledge.

Kohlberg, L. (1984). *The psychology of moral development: The nature and validity of moral stages (Essays on Moral Development, Vol. 2).* New York: Harper & Row.

Mead, G.H. (1913). The social self. *Journal of Philosophy and Scientific Method,* 10: 374–380.

Some, M. (1998). *The healing wisdom of Africa: Finding life purpose through nature, ritual, and community.* New York: Penguin Putnam Inc.

Taubman, P. (1993). Separate identities, separate lives: Diversity in the curriculum. In L.A. Castenell, Jr. and W.A. Pinar (Eds.), *Understanding curriculum as racial text* (pp. 287–306). Albany: State University of New York Press.

Valdes, M.J. (Ed.) (1991). *A Ricoeur reader: Reflection and imagination.* Toronto: University of Toronto Press.

Vedantam S. (2010). *The hidden brain: How our unconscious minds elect presidents, control markets, wage wars, and save our lives.* New York: Spiegel & Grau.

Weissglass, J. (2001, Aug. 8). Racism and the achievement gap. *Education Week.*

Wheatley, M. (2002). *Turning to one another: Simple conversations to restore hope to the future.* San Francisco: Berrett-Koehler Publishers, Inc.

4 | A Conversation of the Head

> We are caught in an inescapable network of mutuality, tied in a single garment of destiny. Whatever affects one directly, affects all indirectly.
>
> (Martin Luther King Jr., *Letters from the Birmingham Jail*)

This is a conversation to uncover the ways in which our "inescapable network of mutuality" has been damaged, making us all victims of racism. This conversation involves our head and includes dynamics that need to be understood by facilitators. A conversation of the heart is one in which participants make statements that often begin with "I feel." One can be confused by how someone feels, can share a different feeling, can even seek more understanding of the feeling, but cannot dismiss the individual's feelings. In contrast, a conversation of the head is one in which an individual begins a statement with "I think." These words can invite debate, proof, support, or justification as reasonable discourse. A conversation of the head, a cognitive domain, is a conversation in which deduction and reasoning are major players while feelings often play a secondary role.

Entering the Conversation

A few facilitative cues can be helpful to insure that this conversation, difficult as it may be, continues and that debate, proof, support, or justification does not silence the dialogue. One cue is to suggest to those school leaders present that for this conversation their challenge is to stay open to new thinking. This is not easy because what we think about racial circumstances is a result of our life experiences and creates a fair amount of certainty. Therefore, we encourage participants to *"suspend certainty"*. Often our thinking is reflected as an either/or proposition. Our propensity to claim an idea as the right one provides us with a sense of security. We defend that idea regardless of other information that would suggest something otherwise. Much like a light switch with only two possibilities—on or off—our cognitive thinking can behave in the same way: right or wrong, agree or disagree, pro or con, on or off.

For this conversation, we encourage participants to give their light switch a "dimmer." There are various degrees of reality. As Parker Palmer reminds us, we really don't live in a world of polarity (one of a light switch with either/or, this or that, yes or no) but instead a world of continuum embracing the possibility of "both/and" (Palmer, 1989). For example, I can unconsciously collude with a system of racism and still be a good person. I can believe that I've worked hard and acknowledge that the system gave me privilege. I can be targeted by a system and not feel that my humanity has been diminished. The "dimmer" switch allows us the advantage of adjusting our certainty. Often our greatest learning emerges from a place that is uncomfortable, unknown, and sometimes a blow to our self-esteem. The light switch with only two choices (on or off) will often inhibit important learning, unlike the dimmer (adjustment) switch which allows a pathway for clarity.

It is also suggested that participants be aware of statements that may silence others. Lisa Delpit explores the idea of silencing the dialogue in

Worksheet 4.1 Statements that Silence the Dialogue

What White people say or do that can silence the dialogue	What People of Color say or do that can silence the dialogue
"Yea, but . . ."	"All White people do this."
*Demand more data.	"This place is so racist."
"There is a perfectly logical explanation."	"My pain is worse than your pain."
"I'm colorblind."	*Only being able to feel or express one emotion such as anger or hopelessness.
"I'm not a racist."	
"Pull yourself up by your bootstraps."	"Let's not air our dirty laundry."
"Don't take it so seriously, lighten up."	*Numbness.
"My best friends are Black."	"I can't trust you."

her research and, simply put, some phrases though said without the intent, will often cause others to "shut down" and withdraw (Delpit, 1995). Worksheet 4.1 explores some common responses and behaviors that will often result in silencing the dialogue. Explore these statements in a full group dialogue. There will be grins and chuckles as we are all guilty at times of these statements. This is where "oops," introduced in Chapter 2, will be rather obvious.

A second way in which this conversation can be embraced and supported comes from a cosmology of African origin—*Ubuntu*. Archbishop Tutu explained Ubuntu as the essence of being human (Tutu, 2004, p. 27).

> Ubuntu speaks particularly about the fact that you can't exist as a human being in isolation. It speaks about our interconnectedness. You can't be human all by yourself, and when you have this quality— Ubuntu—you are known for your generosity. We think of ourselves far too frequently as just individuals, separated from one another, whereas you are connected and what you do affects the whole world. When you do well, it spreads out; it is for the whole of humanity.

Ubuntu provides another concept different from the Cartesian notion of "I think therefore I am." It offers a view of humanity, one of: "I belong therefore I am." This conversation, therefore, is an effort toward understanding how racism interrupts and diminishes our sense of belonging, or in Martin Luther King Jr.'s words, our **"inescapable network of mutuality."**

Common Definition

Beginning this conversation is another opportunity to be transparent regarding definitions. We use the NCCJ definitions established in 1927 for oppression and racism adding visuals representatives (in red) for greater clarity of the definitions in Chapter 3.

> **Oppression:** The one-way systemic mistreatment of a defined group of people, with that mistreatment reinforced and supported by society. (Architecture)

Racism: A complex system of beliefs and behaviors, which are both conscious and unconscious; personal and institutional. They result in the oppression of People of Color and benefit the dominant group. It is a system grounded in the presumed superiority of the White race. (Norm)

Clarifying the Definition

Certainly, time must be spent to discuss these definitions. It is important to remember that these definitions are offered for the purpose of transparency and not an effort to create agreement. It is important for those individuals who might have other ideas regarding oppression and racism that they be given voice for their ideas. This is also a poignant time for the facilitator to benchmark the "dimmer" switch, that there are multiple ways in which we each see reality.

Time also needs to be spent in locating this conversation within institutionalized oppression and racism within the context of the United States. The architecture to be explored is the established laws, customs, and practices in America that support and sustain inequities as well as the unequal distribution of power. Participants should also be reminded that oppressive consequences accrued by laws, customs, or practices do not necessarily reflect individuals who have oppressive intent. If participants view themselves as the "oppressor," it is very likely that this too will only serve to silence their voice. It is helpful to remind individuals that they did not make choices of gender, racial identity, locality, or any other circumstances prior to their birth.

Oppression is experienced as a consequence of, and expressed in, the form of a prevailing conscious and unconscious set of assumptions that defines one group as superior, while another is inferior. No one made a choice of which of these groups would be his/her identity, as examined in the cycle of socialization. Therefore, understanding this architecture of oppression, and in this conversation through a lens of the oppression of racism, is critical work.

Finally, oppression is constructed and impacts each of us in all of the different identities we hold. Therefore, this architecture is applicable to gender, age, socio-economic levels, religion, looks, ability, sexual orientation, etc. Racism is a significant narrative within our country, and holds a significant place within the school setting. In our experience school leaders representing social justice advocacy who understand the architecture of racism, will recognize oppression within other identities. Here again the metaphor of a log jam may be helpful; moving the log of racism empowers others to address other logs, i.e. forms of oppression.

Tables of Oppression

Barbara Love provides an image of oppression as two pillars that support and sustain oppression (Love, 2000, pp. 470–474). The pillars emerge from assumptions of one group having superiority, while another is inferior. Love describes one pillar as the dominant group and the other as the subordinate group. She suggests that in the oppression of racism, White people are cast as members of the group with positions of power. Institutions, as explored in the cycle of socialization, are predominantly owned, organized, and managed by White people. In contrast, the pillar defined as subordinate would be many People of Color who have limited access to positions of power, who are often left out of government, live in substandard housing, are seldom depicted in the media in a positive manner, and are portrayed as welfare recipients, drug addicts, and perpetrators of crime. The role of the dominant group is characterized by bias, beliefs, and behaviors nested in the idea of superiority while the group labeled as subordinate and inferior is targeted by discrimination, stereotyping, limited access to goods, benefits, and resources.

The image of pillars can be somewhat troubling. Pillars are often viewed as indestructible, holding up huge monuments, government buildings, and structures that would seemingly last forever. Pillars are often the image of places of great wealth and power. Therefore, we have found that thinking about these same concepts with the image of a table and table legs is a more accessible image.

Table legs are more easily broken compared to the solid concrete of a pillar. If one table leg is destroyed the table can no longer function. True it may be slanted, but it no longer can serve the purpose for which it was designed. As Love would suggest, table legs, like the pillars, support the oppression of racism. Dominant and subordinate groups are in a symbiotic relationship, i.e. dependent upon each other to hold racism in place. Finally, it is also proposed that the work of dismantling the oppression of racism is work for both groups: Whites and People of Color.

An individual who has been socialized as a member of the dominant group must examine the manner in which power and its corresponding privilege has been provided and sustained. Those who have been socialized as a member of the subordinate group must explore the manner in which they, too, have colluded by unconsciously accepting the distorted image of inferiority. It is critically important to emphasize again that this conversation is not about blame, shame, or guilt. Though those feelings might emerge, they do not lead to understanding, and in a rather subtle way they support the architecture.

The Legs of the Dominant Group

Understanding the legs of dominance must include a vigilant exploration of superiority and privilege. This exploration can easily lead to discomfort, regret, shame, and denial. Educators are not by nature individuals who view themselves as superior. Plenty of evidence exists that educators are "givers," dedicating themselves to the well-being of their students. So as conversations regarding these legs begin, it may be necessary to remind individuals that we are looking at the systemic manner in which oppression is constructed and maintained. Though feelings of shame or guilt may emerge, it is helpful to remind participants that these feelings hold the table in place. Both shame and guilt are personal reactions, and serve only to silence the dialogue regarding the larger institutional reality of racism. Listening pairs as described in Chapter 3 is a way of giving participants a safe place to find words and feelings without judgment. We recommend listening pairs with a simple probe of, "What are you feeling?" This gives individuals opportunity to articulate feelings without judgement and will often diminish levels of anxiety, fear, and confusion.

Exploring superiority should begin with some historical references. Empire makers viewed themselves as the center of the universe and looked upon foreigners as inferior. Ancient Greece and Rome fought wars against those they presumed to be less advanced. This history of dominance and subjection was primarily vested in an exercise of power and strength. Those enslaved were most often captives in war and considered the "bounty" of the battles.

In the sixteenth century a different justification for superiority began with a distortion of the Calvinist ideology of predestination. In this teaching God appointed the eternal destiny of some to salvation by grace, while leaving the remainder to receive eternal damnation for all their sins. Some were believed to be "closer to God" and superior while others were left in damnation for their sins. Although John Calvin never proposed this idea, the Puritans brought with them this hierarchical notion regarding humankind. The pulpit became a voice to support this thinking, i.e. "God Almighty in His most holy and wise providence hath so disposed of the condition of mankind as in all times some must be rich, some poor; some high and eminent in power and dignity, others mean and in subjection" (Griffin, 2000). This theological idea, though wrongly avowed, became a powerful tool for oppression by providing a claim of superiority for some, while subjection for others. It essentially promoted the idea of manifest destiny.

Intersecting with this theological notion was the advancement of capitalism. Mapping the trade winds created a marketplace beyond merely a local setting. Goods that could be grown in one environment could now be transported miles away for consumption in other places. Tobacco, sugar, cotton, indigo, and rice grown in the south would find a lucrative market in England. Capitalism, as a new and global economy, was dependent upon natural resources and labor management. This economic system provided those of superiority and power another justification for targeting those held as inferior in enslavement. It ensured a labor force at no cost and provided great profit and economic gain.

In 1619 the first ship arrived in Jamestown with twenty enslaved Africans. In the same year the House of Burgesses would become the first formation of governance in the Virginia Commonwealth. An economy that was significantly dependent upon the labor force recognized that White indentured servants would eventually gain their freedom, Native Americans could easily hide in a land they knew intimately, but African Americans were easily seen and homeless. The House of Burgesses decreed that the condition of slavery is for life and placed Africans in a different category to White indentured servants (Battalora, 2013). Plantation owners, the elite of the Commonwealth, gained a significant leverage for profit from a free labor force that was now sustained through law.

Bacon's rebellion in 1676 created a strong alliance between enslaved Africans and White indentured servants which threatened the power of the plantation owners. Upon his death and the end of the rebellion, a systematic slave code was adopted. White indentured servants were offered concessions such as lifting taxes, owning land, and the freedom to vote. Enslaved Africans continued to be consider inferior and viewed as personal property, i.e. as a chattel. Superiority was no longer merely an ideology; it had become a significant element in laws which served to dehumanize Africans.

Virginia General Assembly, 1705

All servants imported and brought into the Country . . . who were not Christians in their native Country . . . shall be accounted and be slaves. All Negro, mulatto and Indian slaves within this dominion . . . shall be held to be real estate. If any slave resist his master . . . correcting such slave, and shall happen to be killed in such correction . . . the master shall be free of all punishment . . . as if such accident never happened.

(Griffin, 2000, p. 59)

Additionally, antimiscegenation laws designed to eliminate cross-racial marriage brought "Whiteness" into law. The label "White" as a category of humanity first appeared in 1681 in an antimiscegenation law of the Maryland Commonwealth. Essentially the law's previous use of the term "English or Freeborn" was changed to "White" women. The Virginia Commonwealth enacted a similar prohibition on intermarriage between both White men and White women with "negro, mulatto, or Indian man or woman" in 1691 (Battalora, 2013). White now became a legal racial category.

The false view of superiority grew from a distorted proclamation of religious ideology supported by an overwhelming reliance upon labor as economic leverage and legal bans upon marriage. Though the issue of slavery was without doubt one of controversy and dissent in the beginning stages of the United States, it remained a major element of governance, as identified by the following articles of the Bills of Rights:

- Article 1, Section 2: three-fifths rule for allocation of Congressional representatives (an enslaved individual is counted as three-fifths a person).
- Article 1, Section 9: sanctioned the slave trade for another twenty years.
- Article 4, Section 2: nationalized slavery with the fugitive slave provision.

These historical markers are used to assist White participants to recognize the manner in which even "Whiteness" is a manufactured racial category. Examining the past helps individuals to recognize the cumulative impact upon the present socialization process of messages that are associated with Whiteness. To continue this conversation, use Worksheet 4.2 with all members of this conversation regardless of their individual racial identity. Give participants

Worksheet 4.2 Exploring Whiteness				
What did you hear and learn about Whiteness as you were growing up?				
Family/Friends	*Media*	*Government*	*School*	*Faith-based*

- What messages suggested or implied superiority?
- What were the messages that implied inferiority?
- What meaning do you make of this activity?

time to fill out the following worksheet as individuals. Following a reasonable amount of time, form small groups of no more than four individuals of mixed races to share their worksheets with each other. It will be necessary to remind individuals, as with the cycle of socialization, that individuals did not seek these messages, nor at this point in time do they consciously believe these messages, but these are the messages that impact a sense of identity.

The small groups of mixed race and gender will provide a rich and poignant examination of the differences of the messages each received regarding Whiteness. The conversation also helps each individual develop a deeper understanding of their own social perspective regarding these differences.

Privilege

Establishing a category of dominance and superiority makes the idea of privilege more plausible. After all, if one group is considered to be closer to God, why would it not follow that this same group would have certain privileges, advantages, and entitlements over others? A conversation regarding privilege has become most troubling over the past years. All too often "privilege" has become analogous with elitism. Privilege implies some manipulation or cheating of the system. Most prevalent is a narrow view of privilege as merely a materialistic apparatus. The initial responses to having privilege with a majority of White people include reactions such as: "I grew up poor and had no privilege," "I've worked hard and earned everything I now have," "I don't think of myself as having power, so why would I believe I have privilege?"

Each of these statements has a degree of truth and to simply refute such statements can silence a thoughtful conversation. None of these statements, however, embrace the nature of how privilege and advantage has been extended to the dominant group. Nor do they uncover the institutionalized way in which an oppressive system creates and supports privilege and entitlement. Ironically, these arguments could also be seen as another form of privilege. Dr. Harry Brod, a social justice advocate, provides a significant insight to assist individuals who may be troubled by the discussion of White privilege.

> We need to be clear that there is no such thing as giving up one's privilege to be outside the system. One is always in the system. The only question is whether one is part of the system in a way which challenges or strengthens the status quo.
>
> Privilege is not something I take and which I therefore have the option of not taking. It is something that society gives me, and unless I change the institutions which give it to me, they will continue to give it, and I will continue to have it, however noble and egalitarian my intentions.
>
> (Brod, 1989, in Rothenberg, 2005, p. 104)

Fishbowl

A unique way in which this conversation can be instructive for both White participants and People of Color is to use a fishbowl exercise. Once a culture of respect and safety has been established, this activity is a powerful means of exploring racial consciousness. Use the following narrative as a preface for this activity to reduce any stress or discomfort that may occur.

Fishbowls and Orchestras

Some of you might have been involved in an orchestra as you were growing up. You, of course, know that it is not uncommon for different sections of the orchestra to spend time practicing their own part in isolation from the rest of the group. Thus, the percussion, woodwind, or brass may spend time practicing their unique parts. When sections then re-assemble, the harmony of the music is enhanced because of the opportunity for each section to concentrate on their own individual parts.

Much like an orchestra, for us to truly understand each of the table legs, there are times when we work in separate spaces. This fishbowl is one of the ways in which we learn together in our separate groups. While our White participants unravel privilege, our friends of color are able to observe their work. Much like that of a listening pair, though they might be outside of the circle, our friends of color still are providing attention as they watch their White friends begin to understand the leg of privilege. Later, the fishbowl configuration will be reversed as People of Color will form the center circle to explore the legs of subjection.

Certainly as each individual becomes a part of the inner circle, there may be feelings of discomfort, disconnect, and trepidation. These feelings are real, for none of us seek to be "under a microscope" as the fishbowl image suggests. However, an honest forthright exploration of privilege as members of the dominant group and internalized oppression as members of the target group is critical for our own learning opportunity. Therefore, we again ask people to "lean into the discomfort" as it may be the place in which our most conscious learning takes place.

***At times, someone who is bi-racial might question which group to join. Our experience has been to let the individuals self-select, but we encourage them to think about the way the "world" might treat them as to the distinction between dominance or targeted.

Following this explanation, ask White participants to form the first fishbowl group, with People of Color behind them. Examining the issues of privilege as created and sustained by a system of oppression is a conversation for only those that are cast in that role. This first step also assures People of Color that they are not responsible for teaching White people about issues of racism as is often the pattern. A White facilitator will join the center fishbowl to stimulate conversation. Begin by allowing individuals to express their initial feelings about being in this fishbowl configuration. Often participants will express feelings of discomfort which are characterized by the feeling of disconnect or the idea that this configuration is divisive. Feelings of this nature should not be dismissed, but instead acknowledged. Reminding participants of the orchestra analogy may be helpful. Exploring these feelings also reflects the fact that members of a dominant group are seldom in a position to be observed and perhaps this may indeed be another element of privilege.

Use Worksheet 4.3 as a beginning step for this conversation for those in the inner circle.

Worksheet 4.3 Concept White Privilege

Write in the circles what you know about White privilege.
Add circles if you need to say more.

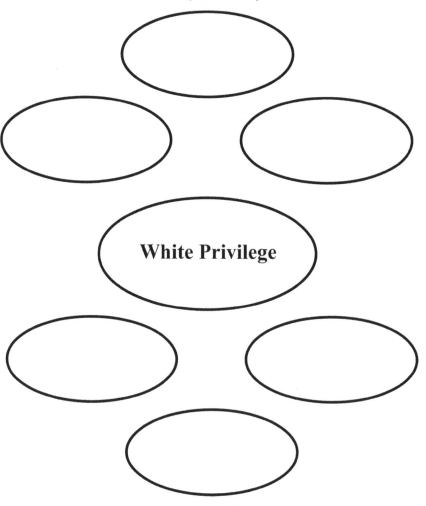

White Privilege

This worksheet gives a context in which privilege is explored by those in the fishbowl. Asking individuals to share and elaborate upon their ideas provides opportunities to explore and broaden the concept of privilege. Many times this concept map will include a number of materialistic responses, e.g. job opportunities, loan approvals, wages, etc. Not surprisingly, this conversation regarding privilege usually begins with the more explicit materialistic gains that "Whiteness" offers individuals. That which is more tangible can be easily identified.

It is in this conversation that individuals may have difficulty identifying privilege because of their own circumstance of poverty or their diligent work effort. Once again, to refute these statements would only raise anxiety and could easily stifle the conversation. Reminding participants of the "dimmer" switch, one that offers the possibility of "both/and" rather than "either/or" is helpful. Being poor or disenfranchised for any number of reasons does not deny the existence of institutionalized privilege. The context of this conversation is to understand a system that provides privilege regardless of an individual's hard work or circumstance of poverty. Maurice Berger offers the following regarding this struggle:

> While other factors might endanger us, our race does not generally threaten our survival or well-being; nor does it provide us with a daily barrage of suspicious glances, physical and emotional evasions, closed doors, and thoughtless comments and insults. Although white people may also be hobbled by prejudice, poverty, or alienation, we can usually count on our whiteness to grant us freer access to a social sphere that is controlled by white people.
>
> (Berger, 1999, p. 168)

Berger's quote helps to examine privilege and entitlement within the nuances of everyday living. In many ways, privilege provides a shield from those "suspicious glances" and "thoughtless comments and insults." Privilege for those in the dominant group becomes subtle, invisible, automatic, and less likely to be considered other than the "norm." The fish is the last to discover the ocean.

To further this context of privilege, we have found Peggy McIntosh's writing entitled *White Privilege: Unpacking the Invisible Knapsack* is most useful. While in the fishbowl configuration, participants are asked to read a few of the statements that highlight privilege as described by McIntosh in the *invisible knapsack* (McIntosh, 1989). It is also important to ask participants to notice what might resonate with them as these statements are read within the circle. The fishbowl exercise for some exposes some vulnerability and there likely may be some tears of shame, guilt, and even sorrow. Here again is the opportunity to use judiciously a listening pair. Remind individuals of the insight from Chapter 2 and Dr. Gray's notion: what we can feel we can heal.

A second activity to use in the fishbowl configuration strengthens the impact of White privilege, in particular within a context that is seldom examined by White people. Ask individuals to share first thoughts regarding each of the probes on Worksheet 4.4:

Worksheet 4.4 Probing White Privilege

How has White privilege impacted . . .

- Where you live?

- Who you socialize with?

- How you cope or heal from pain and adversity in your life?

- Your ability to navigate obstacles in your life?

- Your current economic situation?

- The health care you get?

- The education you received?

- How safe you feel in everyday situations?

How has White privilege impacted . . .

- Your sense of self-esteem and confidence?

- Your sense of your intellectual capacity?

- Your willingness to take risk and make mistakes?

- Your willingness to bend or break rules?

- Your ability to see yourself as a good educator?

How has White privilege impacted . . .

- When planning a lesson?

- Providing interventions for your students?

- Developing a grading scale?

- Structuring or creating discipline policies?

- Interacting with your students?

- Interacting with your students' families?

- Making curricular decisions?

Worksheet 4.4 (Continued)

How has White privilege impacted . . .

- Your willingness to talk about race and racism with People of Color?

- Your willingness to talk about race and racism with other White people?

- Your willingness to confront injustice?

- Your ability to excuse your inaction because of your righteous intention?

The purpose of this fishbowl experience is to open the dialogue for discovering the manner in which superiority and dominance have afforded White people privilege, entitlement, and advantage. As examined in Chapter 3, collusion for any system of oppression is often unconscious. Therefore, this is not an exercise to incite blame or shame, but instead to begin to understand and create a greater consciousness regarding dominance and privilege.

The Legs of the Oppressed

To understand the architecture of the oppression of racism not only do we have to examine the legs of dominance and privilege to ascertain how they hold the oppression of racism in place, but we also have to take an in-depth look at the other two legs that support the oppression of racism. The two legs of targeting and internalized racism need to be explored as well in this activity. These two legs also serve to perpetuate the oppression of racism albeit in a totally different way than the legs of superiority and privilege. The phenomenon of internalized racism occurs when a group of people has been systematically oppressed over a period of time. When people are recipients of repeated discriminatory behavior, a shift in their conscious reality is developed. This shift can cause those targeted to hold limited views about themselves and others in their racial identity group relative to their self-esteem, self-worth, and self-efficacy.

It must be understood that the legs of superiority and privilege create internalized racism and targeting. Paulo Freire uses *prescription* as a way of explaining this condition:

> One of the basic elements of the relationship between oppressor and oppressed is prescription. Every prescription represents the imposition of one individual's choice upon another, transforming the consciousness of the person prescribed to into one that conforms with the

> prescriber's consciousness. Thus, the behavior of the oppressed is a pre-scribed behavior, following as it does the guidelines of the oppressor.
>
> (Freire, 1970, pp. 46–47)

Therefore, what occurs for the formation of these legs of oppression is the repeated targeting by the dominant group of those viewed to be inferior in ways that sustain physical, emotional, and mental hurts. According to Susanne Lipsky, "Black people have been the victims, the primary victims in the country, of every form of abuse, invalidation, oppression and exploitation" (Lipsky, 1987b, p. 144). Joy DeGruy Leary further elucidates this point in her book, *Post Traumatic Slave Syndrome*. She states: "Although slavery has long been a part of human history, American chattel slavery represents a case of human trauma incomparable in scope, duration and consequence to any other incidence of human enslavement" (DeGruy Leary, 2005, p. 75).

One could say, for the most part, that the conditions that would expose African Americans to vicious physical attacks on a day-to-day basis are certainly fewer today than in the past; however, the legacy from those past hurts can still live on in the minds of those so egregiously hurt. This lingering residue can create mental shackles that can often imprison Black people almost as effectively as the leg irons that made physical movement slow and torturous for those who were enslaved. People of Color living in the United States have to battle the racism that is deeply embedded in the fabric of society, as well as the internalized racism, the unconscious shackles, which can keep them in the perpetual loop of self-doubt. Once again, Freire's belief is that this self-doubt or, as he states, self-depreciation, emerges from the internalization of the opinion the oppressors hold of them. Put simply, the *mind* of the oppressed is the tool of the oppressor (Freire, 1970).

Revisiting the Fishbowl Activity

Just as the White participants engage in courageous conversation as they explore issues of dominance and privilege in a fishbowl configuration, People of Color are also invited into a similar configuration. In order to strengthen the culture of respect, safety, and trust, People of Color follow the White fishbowl. Once again, the purpose of this sequence is two-fold: 1) People of Color are often thrust into the role of "educating White people" as to how racism operates in their lives; and 2) it is rewarding for People of

Color to witness the authenticity of their White colleagues as they grapple with teasing into awareness how privilege has provided "the wind in their sails," an observation likely seldom experienced.

As People of Color enter the fishbowl center the facilitator, a Person of Color, joins the group and encourages the participants to share their stories. When members of the group recount how the oppression of racism has pummeled them all of their lives, what often emerges are feelings of both fatigue and pride. Individuals in the People of Color fishbowl will sometimes express feelings of mental and physical exhaustion that can completely overwhelm them, while simultaneously acknowledging their strength and resiliency. As participants talk about their experiences, the facilitator gently nudges them into sharing stories about how internalized racism has created barriers in their lives. A few of the ways in which these barriers can show up are in repeated unworkable relationships with those in one's own identity group, holding lower expectations for those who share their racial identity, and constant thoughts of self-doubt about one's own intelligence. Participants within this fishbowl are frequently reminded that: "Anytime you systematically oppress a group of people that group can internalize that oppression and in turn oppress themselves and other people in their identity group."

As with the other fishbowl, the facilitator should remind participants of no blame, shame, or guilt. People of Color did not construct these legs that would cause them to target themselves and others who look like them. However, what is paramount for the process toward healing is acknowledging the responsibility to shed any invalidating behaviors that reflect patterns of despair and hopelessness. The facilitator of this session encourages the participants to embrace thinking that is liberating and uplifting. Activities to dismantle this oppressive thinking will look different from those of their White counterparts.

One of the exercises that can be employed in this fishbowl activity to promote healing conversation among People of Color is the reading of an essay entitled *Fatigue* by Don Locke. As an anti-racist activist, Locke shares a number of statements representative of behaviors that can cause People of Color to feel both mentally and emotionally exhausted. Statements such as, "I'm tired of dealing with the deadening silence when the conversation turns to race," "I'm tired of hearing White people say that I don't think of you as Black," "I'm tired of being told by White people that I'm too Black and by Black people, I'm not Black enough" are examples of statements that reflect the oppression of racism and internalized racism thinking (Locke, 1994).

Participants are asked to read a statement. Once it is read, they are to pause, reflect, and notice any feelings that might be surfacing as they sit with the experience of that statement.

To make this activity as relevant as possible, individuals within the group are asked to personalize the statement so that it speaks to their particular situation. When feelings do emerge, such as tears or even laughter, the facilitator encourages the individual to "stay with those feelings" because release of this nature is often cathartic. Contrary to popular belief that shedding tears is symbolic of pain, the tears that flow can actually promote healing. During this process, patterns of hopelessness and despair are often recognized as "just patterns" that do not mirror the personal power, self-efficacy, and nobility of those individuals who are sharing.

Another activity that may be used in the fishbowl setting is an open conversation about a quiet consciousness that People of Color constantly carry. Similar to Don Locke's essay, Worksheet 4.5 features statements that reflect a kind of "heaviness" that People of Color carry throughout their lives. Once again, individuals are asked to share their responses to these probes. Feelings manifesting themselves as tears or even laughter will once again surface, and as in the previous activities, the facilitator helps participants to recognize the pattern and remind participants that these patterns do not define or diminish their humanity.

Worksheet 4.5 Probing Internalized Oppression

When will the time come when . . .

- I will trust my own brilliant thinking?

- White people will not be surprised by my brilliant thinking?

- My heart will not automatically beat faster out of fear when a police car happens to be behind me?

- I won't have to second guess whether White people are responding to me on the basis of my being African American or on the basis of the subject matter being discussed?

- I won't be profiled without any provocation or justification?

- A mistake that is made by one Person of Color won't be viewed by other People of Color as an embarrassment reflecting upon all members of that group?

- I won't have to prove to other People of Color in my group that I embrace my identity with just as much authenticity as they do (Black, Latino/ Latina, Japanese, Chinese . . .)?

Invite the participants to add their voice to this exercise.

As was stated, the work that must be done with White people regarding the legs of dominance includes a much different dynamic than the work of People of Color who are exploring their legs of oppression. Not surprisingly, the fatigue activity can easily create a sense of tiredness and to some degree cause participants to feel a sense of self-doubt or resonate with the thought of "when will it ever end." To assist People of Color in ridding themselves of the "prescriptions" that have been foisted upon them by the targeting, a final activity is used in this fishbowl configuration. Participants are asked to respond to a series of questions posed by Suzanne Lipsky (1987a). This activity is purposely designed to mitigate the negative thinking constantly swirling in and around People of Color. Individuals are asked to respond to the following statements and blank spaces in the questions are for the various ethnicities that reflect the People of Color group.

- What's good about being _____?
- What makes you proud of being _____?
- What are _____ people really like?
- What's difficult about being _____?
- What do I want other people to know about me?
- When do I remember being supported by another _____?
- When do I remember acting on some feeling of internalized oppression?

A final conversation within the fishbowl configuration would examine how individuals can continue to eradicate feelings originating from internalized racism thinking. As in the preceding activity, participants are reminded to repeatedly reflect upon their goodness and the goodness of others.

Continuing Conversations

As suggested with a conversation of the heart, this conversation is by no means completed by these exercises. For some participants this may be the first time racism has been presented in this manner. Understanding racism within this architecture of oppression must therefore be a continuing conversation. White participants may have never engaged in this careful examination of privilege. In the same manner, participants of color may have never considered the internalization of racism. Consequently, social justice leaders need to plan intentional opportunities for participants engaged in this work to come together for further conversation. One configuration for these additional conversations could be race caucus groups.

Caucus Groups: A Process for Reflection

A caucus group is formed by individuals who share the same racial identity. A race caucus group of this nature may seem divisive. However, there are times when both groups need a safe space for examining their individual issues. The fishbowl is an instructive way of exploring the table legs of oppression. However the fishbowl still places folks in a space that might not offer as much comfort and safety as the caucus arrangement. Educators are often individuals who are keenly aware of others' feelings. Consequently, the openness of voicing issues regarding racism, even in the fishbowl configuration, may be tempered as to not offend others. With little doubt civility regarding this conversation is of great value, but so too is honesty. The opportunity for Whites and People of Color to express confusion, challenge dispositions, and clarify elements of their particular table leg without a need to filter words or phrases is critical for learning.

A caucus configuration provides a space for this kind of open, forthright dialogue to exist. It is also a configuration that helps people who share a similar position of either dominance or subjection to learn from each other. Creating a conversation within a caucus group may result from merely asking individuals: "What might you have discovered in the fishbowl? What might you still be struggling with regarding the fishbowl conversation?" Keeping this conversation organic without a prescribed agenda is usually sufficient for this kind of reflection. The importance of this continuing conversation in a caucus configuration is to gather insights from others as a forum for self-discovery. Once again, as Margaret Wheatley suggested: **"Conversation is the natural way in which humans think together."**

Final Comment: Transference

As stated at the beginning of this chapter, these exercises and activities have all been focused on the oppression of racism. Their applicability to any other form of oppression is valid. Courageous conversations regarding other oppressions will require a similar exploration of a dominant group with power and privilege and a targeted group experiencing targeting and internalized oppression. This diligent effort to understand the architecture of the oppression of racism provides individuals with the knowledge and willingness to explore all other oppressions that exist in schools and classrooms.

References

Battalora, J. (2013). *Birth of a white nation: The invention of white people and its relevance today,* Houston, TX: Strategic Book Publishing and Rights Co.

Berger, M. (1999). *White lies: Race and the myth of whiteness.* New York: Farrar, Straus and Giroux.

Brod, H. (1989). Work clothes and leisure suits: The class basis and bias of the men's movement. In M. S. Kimmel and M. Messner (Eds.), *Men's Lives.* New York: Macmillan.

DeGruy Leary, J. (2005). *Post traumatic slave syndrome: America's legacy of enduring injury and healing.* Milwaukie, OR: Uptone Press.

Delpit, L. (1995). *Other people's children: Cultural conflicts in the classroom.* New York: The New Press.

Freire, P. (1970). *Pedagogy of the oppressed.* New York: Continuum Publishing Company.

Griffin, P. (2000). *Seeds of racism in the soul of America.* Naperville, IL: Sourcebooks Inc.

Lipsky, S. (1987a). *Black re-emergence.* Seattle, WA: Rational Island Publishing.

Lipsky, S. (1987b). *Revaluation counseling.* Seattle, WA: Rational Island Publishing.

Locke, D. (1994). Fatigue: An essay. Adapted and reprinted by permission of the author, Don C. Locke.

Love, B. (2000). Developing a liberatory consciousness. In M. Adams, W. J. Blumenfield, R. Castaneda, H. W. Hackman. M. L. Peters and X. Zuniga (Eds.), *Readings for diversity and social justice* (2nd ed., pp. 470–474). New York: Routledge.

McIntosh, P. (1989). *White privilege: Unpacking the invisible knapsack.* Wellesly, MA: Peace and Freedom.

Palmer, P. (1989) T*he courage to teach: Exploring the inner landscape of a teacher's life.* San Francisco: Jossey-Bass.

Rothenberg, P. (2005). *White privilege: Essential readings on the other side of racism.* New York: Worth Publishers.

Tutu, D. (2004). *God has a dream: A vision of hope for our time.* New York: Double Day.

Wheatley, M. (2002). *Turning to one another: Simple conversations to restore hope to the future.* San Francisco: Berrett-Koehler Publishers, Inc.

A Conversation
of the Hand

We often confuse dialogue *as* anti-racism rather than as what prepares or organizes us *for* anti-racism.

(Paul Gorski, 2008)

Entering the Conversation

The preceding conversations on personal stance and knowledge regarding oppression, and in a more direct manner the oppression of racism, are a necessary precursor to the adoption of strategies to confront injustices within the school setting. As Gorski suggests, these conversations are merely the beginning steps not the destination (Gorski, 2008, pp. 32–36). Therefore, this conversation is centered upon the question: what do we now do?

In the Classroom

In *Affirming Diversity*, Sonia Nieto writes that culturally responsive teaching is one in which students' identities are recognized, respected, and used as meaningful sources for creating optimal learning environments. Strategies of instruction for optimal learning environments emanate from instructional activities to master skills/knowledge and promote/support a strong sense of belonging for each student (Nieto, 1996). This term "belonging" can be examined effectively by using the following attributes: **safety, value, power, dignity, and self-actualization**. Begin this conversation by having school leaders fill out Worksheet 5.1 as individuals and then form small groups to share thoughts.

This worksheet can stimulate a more in-depth reflection upon social justice strategies within the classroom to support culturally responsive teaching.

Worksheet 5.1 Attributes of Belonging

Attribute	How do you create and sustain this attribute?
Safety	
Value	
Power	
Dignity	
Self-actualization	

What follows are sample activities for this conversation for each of the five attributes.

Safety

A young Latina girl shared a poignant thought regarding her sense of safety in the classroom when, participating in a fishbowl, she said this to the surrounding teachers:

> *"You think your classroom is safe because you are safe."*

The statement was not an indictment upon teachers but certainly provides a perspective regarding safety that ought to be considered. How is

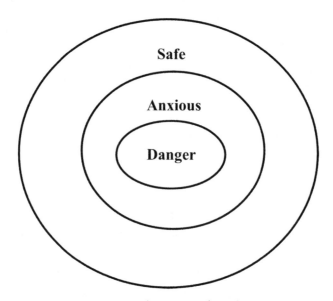

Figure 5.1 Floor Survey for Safety

safety viewed by students of very different backgrounds and life experiences? Clearly, students who are experiencing success in school seek a sense of safety more centered upon academic expectations and evaluation criteria. Students who have had less success and have been disenfranchised from the system will be seeking safety that reflects acceptance, respect, and worthiness. Place tape or yarn on the floor to represent three concentric circles with specific descriptors for each circle as shown in Figure 5.1.

Merely asking students to respond to various questions of safety by stepping into the circle that best represents their feelings can lead to insights regarding the needs of students. Questions, of course, can be modified depending upon the age of students and can cover a wide range of contexts, for example:

- How do you feel about raising your hand to answer a question?
- How do you feel about being wrong?
- How do you feel about name calling?
- How do you feel about talking about your background or life experiences?
- How do you feel about taking risks?
- How do you feel about speaking in a large group/a small group?

This activity also allows students to see the feelings of other classmates. Often a level of safety is felt when individuals recognize that others may feel the same way regarding these questions. Depending upon the developmental age of the students, questions such as these can also stimulate conversations between students regarding feelings, thus providing a more socially inclusive culture within the classroom.

A variety of applications of this circle activity can be accomplished by merely changing the words. Using words like "agree, disagree, no opinion" or "feel, think, do" or "really ready, not quite ready, not ready" offers a number of different contexts for using this visual upon a floor. It allows students to express themselves in a unique manner and provides teachers with an observation of the variety of perspectives held by their students.

Another consideration a social justice school leader should make is the research regarding stereotype threat. Claude Steele and Joshua Aronson (1995) explored this condition by defining stereotype threat as the threat of being viewed through the lens of a negative stereotype, or the fear of doing something that would inadvertently confirm that stereotype, and how that might impact academic performance (Perry, Steele, and Hilliard III, 2003). They designed experiments to test whether the performance of students who are aligned with a stereotype of diminished intellectual prowess (a narrative of African American students) would ultimately be impacted compared with students who are not stereotyped in the same manner. In all of their experiments these students performed poorly when compared with White students, at times a full standard deviation below their counterparts. To further explore this concept, they told White male students that they would be taking a difficult math test on which Asian students generally do better than Whites. White male students who do not have a stereotype of group inferiority and were academically equal in math ability, performed significantly poorer than their Asian counterparts. They explored the same conditions with regard to gender with the same results between men and women. After numerous other experiments of a similar kind, their conclusions were that even in groups that are not generally stereotyped as inferior, performance was impacted and diminished.

This research promoted the idea of "identity safety," i.e. one in which the classroom teacher is intentional regarding ability affirmation coupled with high standards. A culturally responsive classroom is one in which a student's identity is recognized, respected, and appreciated. Without that respect a student may feel a major loss of self and regard the only alternative to be not to learn and to reject the world (Kohl, 1967).

Value

There is no doubt that we all seek and ultimately need a sense of value within our environments. Students' seeking a sense of value in the school must do so in an environment where competition plays a major role. Education must prepare students in ways that will allow them to compete in the world of economics, occupation, and social structure. However, competition also creates a culture of winners and losers and competition in schools is ubiquitous. Athletics is an obvious player and for some schools athletic prowess becomes a dominant attribute of one's identity. Academics play an equal role in this culture of competition as in grade distribution, class eligibilities, college entrance exams, and "ranking" criteria for awards and recognition.

Seeking a sense of value for students who perform well in this competitive environment is much less problematic than for students who have been disenfranchised, marginalized, and devalued. For these students, a sense of value emerges predominantly through the relationships experienced within the school with teachers and other students. For this reason, promoting a sense of value for students experiencing targeting from oppression must include an authentic, genuine, and trusting relationship.

Creating a classroom environment where students feel a sense of value is established through the type of social culture reflected in the classroom. This, of course, requires instructional practices that are benchmarked by a pedagogy of cooperative learning. Clearly there is evidence to support cooperative learning as an excellent instructional practice to achieve effective academic performance. Equally important is that cooperative learning provides a reasonable balance with competition. In a classroom where appropriate elements of cooperative learning are used frequently, the social structure of the classroom becomes a community of *learners* rather than a community of *competitors*.

Johnson and Johnson's work regarding cooperative learning includes both the attributes of positive interdependence—the manner in which members of a cooperative group recognize their dependence upon each other—and individual accountability—the manner in which each member of a cooperative group has an individual responsibility to each member of the group (Johnson and Johnson, 2009). These two elements begin to grow a classroom culture where each child has a sense of value that is not solely reliant upon performance. It also suggests that each individual student's voice has value and contributes to the learning process within this community. Cooperative learning also supports what Gloria Ladson-Billings calls for regarding culturally responsive instruction:

> Encouraging a community of learners means helping students work against the norm of competitive individualism. The teachers believe that the students have to care, not only about their own achievement but also about their classmates' achievement.
>
> (Ladson-Billings, 1994, p. 69)

Many teachers are aware of cooperative learning strategies and the following protocol for grading will promote conversations regarding the development of students' caring about not only their own achievement, but their classmates' as well.

Grading Protocol

In preparation for any learning concept a cooperative group can be formed. Cooperative groups of three students are encouraged: students who are reasonably close in academic ability and/or preparation, and students who the teacher knows have the social skills to be able to function in a cooperative group setting. Cooperative groups should also understand positive interdependence and individual accountability, principles that have been introduced and practiced as a part of the classroom environment.

Explain to the students what is expected of them regarding this concept and what will be assessed at the end of the learning period. Explain also that the final assessment will be given individually, but if the cooperative learning group's collective scores is above a certain criteria, each member of the group will receive additional bonus points to be added to their individual score.

Give students Worksheet 5.2.

Worksheet 5.2 Grading Protocol

Concept—Pythagorean Theorem

Assessment criteria: Know the theorem and its resulting axioms on final test

20 point test

3 bonus points for a collective score above 48 points

Scoring procedure for each cooperative group: Example

Cooperative Group	Individual Score +	Bonus Score	= Grade Book Score
Alex	17	3	20
Stacy	15	3	18
Dominique	18	3	21
Collective Score	50		above 48 bonus point criterion

This profile for grading has subtle ways in which a classroom becomes a community of learners. The bonus point feature regarding grades promotes the value of each member of the cooperative group as a meaningful contributor for academic success. A grade for cooperative learning activities should never be the average grade of the cooperative group. This bonus feature allows additional points for each member and not at the risk of their own individual effort. Finally, the bonus point is also a statement to the students by their teacher, that she or he values their participation in the learning environment.

Along with cooperative learning, much has been written about the notion of mirrors and windows within literature. The value of students "seeing" themselves as in a mirror is without question a valuable attribute of literacy instruction. Conversely, a student whose literature provides only a window into someone else's reality diminishes their engagement as well as a feeling of value.

> When children cannot find themselves reflected in the books they read, or when the images they see are distorted, negative, or laughable, they learn a powerful lesson about how they are devalued in the society of which they are a part.
>
> (Bishop, 1990, p. 557)

Another important conversation regarding value is centered upon how all students within the classroom and school see accurate representations of themselves. Who is looking at mirrors and who is looking through windows is an important conversation regarding a student's value. Use Worksheet 5.3 for teachers to engage in this exploration and promote a variety of identities, e.g. race, gender, socio-economic, etc.

Worksheet 5.3 Mirrors and Windows

Students' identity	What mirrors exist in your classroom	What windows exist in your classroom

The effort for students, all students, to have a strong sense of value results from the relationships that exist between the teacher and the student. Exploring ways in which instructional practices can serve this effort is worthy of conversation. It is clear that the cooperative grading protocol has limitations and for some educators it will not be considered a reasonable procedure. However, this grading protocol profile and the exploration of "mirrors and windows" may serve as a catalyst for educators to explore the manner in which their instructional practices can highlight the value of each student.

Power

There is no doubt that power within the classroom lies with the teacher. Teachers have the power of establishing classroom norms, determining learning activities, deciding grades, evaluating student progress, monitoring behavior, and a myriad of other activities that rest solely upon his or her discretion. No one would argue that this kind of power is inappropriate and though there have been circumstances of individuals misusing this power to hurt students, those exceptions do not justify a shift of this power. Schools must be places of civility and the power to create and sustain that civility must stay under the purview of the teachers and administrators. Additionally, students' input, as advocates rather than adversaries, should be sought in this effort to create civility within the classroom. Based upon creating this inclusive culture within the classroom, teachers must seek ways in which students are empowered.

Exploring this possibility begins, we believe, with a distinction between power and empowerment. Power is reflected in domination, control, and essentially authority "over" people, processes, procedures, and decisions. In this respect power is afforded individuals from outside sources as in certifications, licensure, position, credential, etc. Empowerment can be viewed as power "within" a disposition, attitude, feeling, and belief about self. In this way, empowerment is not dependent upon an outside source to validate, confirm, or legitimize.

Given this perspective, we would suggest that empowerment of students results from a relationship of co-agency, one in which the relationship between teacher and student is redefined. This relationship emerges as teachers reject the notion of "banking education," one described by Paulo Freire, in which students learn to regurgitate and passively accept the knowledge they are handed (Freire, 1970). In contrast, a relationship of co-agency is one in which student and teacher problem solve together. The effort in this relationship is to provide students the opportunity to be curious, to question, and to become problem solvers.

The Center for Education, Diversity, and Excellence (CREDE) offers a set of instructional standards that reflect this co-agency dimension calling for teaching through conversation. The following is its description of this standard:

> This concept may appear to be a paradox: instruction implies authority and planning, while conversation implies equality and responsiveness. But the instructional conversation is based on assumptions that are fundamentally different from those of traditional lessons.
>
> Teachers, who use it, like parents in a natural teaching setting, assume that the student has something to say beyond the known answers in the head of the adult. The adult listens carefully, makes guesses about the intended meaning, and adjusts responses to assist the student's efforts—in other words, engages in conversation.
>
> Such conversation reveals the knowledge, skills, and values—the culture—of the learner, enabling the teacher to contextualize teaching to fit the learner's experience base.

Use Worksheet 5.4 for teachers to reflect upon instructional practices that serve to create, support, and sustain this instructional strategy. Form small groups after individuals have completed this worksheet for further conversations.

Worksheet 5.4 Teacher Practices

Teacher Practices	1	2	3	4	5
	Seldom			Frequently	
Arrange the classroom to accommodate conversation between the teacher and a small group of students on a regular and frequent basis.					
Has a clear academic goal that guides conversation with students.					
Ensures that student talk occurs at higher rates than teacher talk.					

(Continued)

Worksheet 5.4 (Continued)

Teacher Practices	1	2	3	4	5
	Seldom			**Frequently**	
Guides conversation to include students' views, judgments, and rationales using text evidence and other substantive support.					
Ensures that all students are included in the conversation according to their preferences.					
Listens carefully to assess levels of students' understanding.					
Assist students' learning throughout the conversation by questioning, restating, praising, encouraging, etc.					
Guides the students to prepare a product that indicates the instructional conversation's goals were achieved.					

Student empowerment is also achieved when one considers the opportunity students have for choices within the classroom. Another conversation regarding this variable can be created after using Worksheet 5.5.

Professional development regarding instructional practice is enhanced when teachers have time to reflect upon practice. These worksheets can stimulate the opportunity for teachers to compare and contrast their various instructional practices regarding power within their classroom setting.

Dignity

Parsing out dignity as a separate, individual attribute to be examined within the context of instructional practice creates again the redefining of the

Worksheet 5.5 Choices Students Can Make

Choices my students can make regarding instruction	Choices my students can make regarding curriculum	Choices my students can make regarding behavior

relationship experienced by teacher and student. A culturally responsive environment is one in which each student's identity is treated with dignity. Put another way, a responsive environment for students is one in which the teacher sees and believes that each child is a "dignified" person. To be seen as a dignified member of a classroom is yet another element of belonging. When "children feel they belong and find their realities reflected in the curriculum and conversations of schooling, research has demonstrated repeatedly that they are more engaged in learning and that they experience greater school success" (Shields, 2004, p. 122). Thus, individual teacher "stance" emerges once again as the major contributor to that belief. Consequently, when considering a culturally responsive classroom environment, the teacher is the lesson plan.

Assisting students in their efforts to be curious, to question, and to become problem solvers involves a constant dialogue between teachers and students. A teacher's response to students can be viewed as a significant measure of whether that teacher treats students with dignity. Our word choices do more than convey thinking; words also convey feelings. Paradoxically, the absence of words provides little for meaning, but can be seen as a message of invisibility, dismissiveness, and ambivalence.

Exploring the manner in which we respond to students is worthy of our time, and may unravel unconscious beliefs regarding students different from ourselves. Use this worksheet as one way to brainstorm statements for correcting students without the cost of their dignity.

Words, as Freire suggest, do not describe the world, instead they *define* the world (Freire, 1970). Our school language is filled with words that describe students and subsequently, in Freire's thinking, these words also *define* students. When working with schools that are involved with a voluntary transfer program in which students from the inner city are transported to

Worksheet 5.6 Saying Wrong in a Positive Manner

Ways you can say wrong in a positive manner
Example: "I like your thinking because you were using prior knowledge and your answer isn't what I was looking for."
1
2
3
4

suburban school settings, we often hear teachers and administrators use the term "city kids." This term becomes equivalent to creating an unconscious narrative about these students; usually as poor, of questionable moral family structure, Black, and lacking motivation and/or intellectual capacity.

The culturally sensitive classroom must be mindful of the manner in which students come to know themselves. Theresa Perry, in *Young, Gifted, and Black,* refers to this "knowing of oneself" as a narrative established in our schools, neighborhoods, through the media, and also within faith-based dispositions regarding students. Similar to Taubman's fictional register, as stated earlier, students can be held victim by these narratives. Theresa Perry suggests that what we need in schools is a "counternarrative," one that confronts the messages surrounding our young people about their intellect and capacity for learning (Perry et al., 2003).

We often hear the term "at-risk" students, and though that term serves a purpose in providing students with the kinds of interventions that will support their growth, it carries an unconscious narrative that can often impact expectations. One participant suggested the term of "at-promise" as a way of confronting that narrative which also honors the need for intervention. Use Worksheet 5.7 as an exercise in "rewriting" a number of terms used in school that can often assault a student's sense of dignity. Once again, this worksheet serves as a catalyst for a deeper conversation regarding efforts to create a culturally responsive school environment where each student feels a strong sense of belonging.

Worksheet 5.7 Counternarratives

What could be a counternarrative to these narratives?

1. At-risk student   _____
2. Marginal learner   _____
3. Discipline problem   _____
4. Minority   _____
5. City kids   _____
6. Doesn't care   _____
7. Achievement gap   _____
8. _____   _____
9. _____   _____
10. _____   _____

Self-actualization

Walk into just about any Kindergarten classroom in the country and you will likely see on the walls numerous charts; charts that plot a variety of numbers, sizes, colors, shapes, etc. Charts that show the daily incremental growth of the plant that started as a small seed in a Dixie cup. Kindergarten teachers are notorious for finding ways to make learning visual and fluid. Five-year-olds are usually surrounded with a number of ways in which they can see and know they are learning "something." Of course, this classroom environment shifts as students progress through grades, and for many students that visual, frequent view of their own growth becomes fragmented and often disconnected from their own "lived lives." We all tend to learn material that has meaning in the context of our own lives, sometimes without even trying. What about students who have "lived lives" different from our own? Clearly the lived experiences of students of color, a targeted group, are much different from that of White students, a privileged group.

Consider the following research by Rosalyn Mickelson that compared abstract attitudes and lived experiences (Mickelson, 2008). She found stronger levels of agreement among Black students compared with White students when asked about "abstract" values regarding education such as:

- Education is the key to success in the future.
- If everyone in America gets a good education, we can end poverty.
- Getting a good education is a practical road to success.
- Education will really pay off for me.
- I have a chance of making it if I do well in school.
- Achievement and effort in school lead to job success later on.

When Black students were asked about "lived experiences" regarding education, responses included the following:

- Although my parents tell me to get a good education to get a good job, they face barriers to job success.
- People in my family haven't been treated fairly at work, no matter how much education they have.
- Studying in school rarely pays off later with good jobs.
- Based on their experiences, my parents say people like us are not always paid or promoted according to our education.

Though Blacks expressed greater agreement than Whites regarding the abstract results of education, their concrete attitudes (their lived lives) are less hopeful and imply doubts regarding fairness. Connecting lesson planning to include how content is connected to the "lived lives" of students is not a simple endeavor. But the absence of that connection does impact the degree to which students are engaged. We all learn more when the learning is intricately woven into the manner in which we live our lives.

Another aspect to consider when exploring a sense of self-actualization is the degree to which a student understands the lesson. Ronald Ferguson's research, which involved seventh and eleventh grade students across racial identities regarding student engagement, provided the following data with respect to understanding the lesson (Ferguson, 2008). When he asked students the percentage of time they *completely understood* the teacher's lesson, the following responses were reported:

About 50% or less				
Black	*White*	*Hispanic*	*Asian*	*Mixed Race*
48%	28%	46%	31%	38%

This data would promote a number of strategies that teachers can use to assess student understanding more intentionally during the lesson presentation. One suggestion from a number of middle and high school teachers is to provide **a note card** for each student at the beginning of a period. At the end of the period, simply ask students to write whatever questions they might still have regarding the instruction on one side and how teaching this could improve. This note card essentially affords a student who has been marginalized the opportunity to ask a question and not risk embarrassment or place at risk his/her dignity and, at the same time, provide the teacher with important feedback regarding instructional practice. It also provides a kind of "power" by soliciting improvement for the teacher and even a sense of "value"—my ideas are important.

Further Conversations

Using the attributes of safe, value, power, dignity, and self-actualization has proven to be a productive manner of exploring the "hand" within the classroom. Positive professional development for teachers is best served when opportunity exists for teachers to share, compare, contrast, and elaborate upon their own practices.

In the School

Unlike in the classroom where the onus of responsibility for a culturally responsive classroom is with the teacher, for the school it becomes a collective responsibility of the entire professional staff, each to serve as a social justice advocate. It is the long shadows of the adults within the building that creates the culture within the school. Leadership is hinged therefore upon creating a shared vision for that "shadow."

This book is a template for courageous conversations regarding social justice leadership using the head, heart, and hands. Social justice leaders must also recognize that this kind of reform is one of a second-order change. A second-order change is not incremental. It is a dramatic departure from the norm and alters the system in fundamental ways, requiring new thinking and behavior. In the book *School Leadership that Works*, the authors provide important considerations regarding a second-order change (Marzano, McNulty and Waters, 2007). In this work, twenty-one principal's responsibilities were explored as to their impact upon student achievement. The research also highlighted four of those responsibilities that support change efforts. **Culture** is one of those responsibilities and leadership in this area is defined as: an effective leader builds a culture that positively influences teachers, who, in turn positively influence students. **Communication** is a critical feature of any endeavor in school reform efforts. As suggested in earlier chapters of this book, a "both/and" rationale supports the staff to explore dispositions, attitudes, and feelings regarding this cultural change. **Order**, efforts to create a culturally responsive school environment, is seldom linear. Thus, attention must be paid to both the personal and professional needs of the staff. Finally, **input** must be authentic and timely. Helping staff to recognize their own individual growth contributes to the collective "ownership" needed for this second-level change.

Consider Readiness

This book is rooted in a "healing" conversation in order to create change. As has been stated, our efforts emerge from a belief that we have all been hurt by racism and other oppressions, and our efforts to listen while others heal is critical for this journey. Individuals will enter this journey based upon their own lived experience. As such, every individual will bring his/her own sense of identity, conscious and unconscious socialization, and life experiences that create a myriad of understanding regarding oppression. Perhaps the metaphor of a parking lot is useful in thinking about the readiness of a professional staff to begin this journey: see Worksheet 5.8.

Everyone within a school setting may indeed arrive at issues of social justice like our imaginary parking lot and behave in a similar manner as described above. Spending time therefore, to explore the readiness of staff to address these issues is most advisable. Dr. Frances E. Kendall provides an excellent instrument to assess this readiness. She poses a number of probes regarding the seriousness of the school to address the issue of diversity, the language used when discussing diversity, and the place and who is talking about diversity. The Kendall survey provides a lens through which school leaders can begin

Worksheet 5.8 The Parking Lot Metaphor

The Parking Lot

Picture a parking lot with spaces to park and some labeled specifically for people living with a disability. Many drivers will respect this label and park somewhere else on the lot. However, others may ignore the label, justifying their parking with the idea that they will only be a short time in the store. This image offers us three levels of thinking about social justice leadership.

The first of these levels is the fact that the construction of the parking lot includes an acknowledgement of the need for some to have closer access to the entrance. Much like public education we acknowledge different needs in formal ways, e.g. special education, gifted programs, AP courses.

A second level of thinking is exemplified by those who arrive at our imaginary parking lot respecting the needs of different individuals and choosing to park in other spaces. This is much like many educators who respect the various learning needs of the students and adjust instruction to accommodate their needs.

A final level of thinking is one of either denial or oblivion. This would be those who arrive at the parking lot and ignore the label, park their car in the space, and go about their business. Neil Postman (Postman and Weingartner, 1969) suggested that public education is guilty of a "carry on regardless" nuance. This level reflects that "carry on" dynamic and as well, the dysfunction of a "colorblind" stance that ignores significant data that indicates inequity. This level may emerge from a blatant denial of difference, but more likely, it results from a lack of a critical consciousness regarding social justice issues.

conversations regarding oppressions and the eventual creation of an inclusive, culturally responsive school environment (www.franceskendall.com).

This work must become embedded in the daily work of the school. As such, one consideration for the school setting is to identify data that can be accumulated which demonstrates progress. Data is needed to guide progress, and though data regarding an affective domain is "slippery," it should not be ignored.

In one central Illinois large urban school district of over 6000 students, the principal of a middle school shared the following regarding his leadership role to support social justice advocacy:

> The foundation for social justice advocacy must be embedded in the vision of the leader. Moving along a continuum toward cultural competence needs to be a part of the climate of the school. This is accomplished through education and training (head), deepened relationships (heart), and action (hands).

This school includes a student population that is 60 percent Caucasian and 38 percent African American, and 57 percent of students are eligible for Free and Reduced Lunches. The principal benchmarked the essential connection between the personal journey and professional practice through data collected for the Positive Behavioral Intervention and Support Program (PBIS).

PBIS is a national program which identifies disciplinary action in ways that are uniform, consistent, and effective. Collection of this data over time helps staff members to recognize effective intervention strategies, inconsistencies of practice, and development of a stronger focus upon students in greatest need of intervention. This was the "natural" data used by the principal to help staff recognize the disproportionality of race in office referrals.

One item used in the assessment of teachers from the National Center for Culturally Responsive Educational Systems asks, **"Is the teacher aware of how his/her own racial identity affects his/her assessment of the student?"** (NCCRESt, 2005). One's own racial identity can also affect disciplinary referrals to the office. Research data (which will be included in the next chapter) asserted that Black boys were referred to the office more often as an interpretation of behavior rather than an explicit breaking of a rule.

The principal was able to involve 90 percent of the staff in conversations as outlined in this book. He then used PBIS data to support the effort toward racial consciousness within his staff. Through sharing and examining discipline data by categories of behaviors (i.e. "subjective" categories such as defiance, disrespect, and disruption), school staff were able to affect a 37 percent decrease in subjective referrals for all students from 2006–07 to 2008–09. Additionally, over a four-year period, the data also included a significant reduction of referrals for special education testing from 2.6 percent to 0.1 percent. This reduction at a middle school level is of significant importance as Black males remain disproportionately identified for special education. Finally as indicated by the data, fewer referrals to the office meant increased instructional engagement, which is no doubt a major element of reducing the achievement gap. As suggested for classrooms, this principal provided a means in which growth particularly in the affective domain of stance could be viewed and account for the positive results.

Another School-Wide Effort: Evaluation

Within the school setting, one manner in which every professional is "touched" by the system is evaluation. For most schools throughout the country, a clinical evaluative process is conducted for teachers. The steps of this process include a pre-conference prior to a classroom observation, the classroom observation, and a post-conference to discuss the observation with constructive feedback for improvement. In one district in which social justice advocacy was a high priority, the administration created the following profile for the formal classroom observation. The numerical statements are the questions raised and the corresponding evidence of teaching behavior to support the statement.

1. **How does the teacher inquire about the students' school and life experiences that will impact their learning regarding this lesson?**
   - The teacher demonstrates thorough knowledge of students' backgrounds, cultures, level of development, skills, and interests, and uses this knowledge to plan for individual student learning.
   - The teacher connects the lesson plan to the experiences and prior knowledge of all students.
   - The teacher shows a respect and appreciation for various/diverse cultural backgrounds.

2. **How has the lesson, or the lesson plan, addressed the nature of the learning task for diverse cultures?**

    - The teacher includes a (wide) range of tasks/activities to engage the diversity of experiences among all students.

    - The lesson plan or implemented lesson can be connected to the prior experiences of students in terms of gender, culture, race, or socioeconomic status.

3. **What are you noticing or asking yourself regarding student talk?**

    - The teacher has created a culture that allows students to honor everyone's (other's) voice(s).

    - The teacher has established expectations/respect for active listening and participation among students.

    - The teacher allows student talk to guide the lesson and uses it to enrich instruction.

4. **What are you noticing or asking yourself regarding student participation?**

    - The teacher creates a climate in which mistakes are opportunities for learning and student participation strengths are emphasized with "wait time."

    - The teacher develops ways to involve all students in the lesson.

    - The teacher monitors student engagement.

5. **What are you noticing about the manner in which the teacher attends to the students?**

    - The teacher circulates using proximity to provide assistance discreetly.

    - The teacher utilizes Bloom's Taxonomy when developing creative questioning techniques.

    - The teacher has a knowledge of providing opportunities for student-led discussion and how much time is spent on "teacher talk."

6. **What are you noticing about the tone of the teacher's voice, the choice of words, what is stressed, and how information is retaught?**

    - The teacher begins the lesson with a positive statement so students are apt to be more engaged in a lesson or activity.

- The teacher maintains a non-threatening, positive tone of voice when addressing and engaging students.
- The teacher's voice and choice of words reflect high expectations for all students.

7. **During the post-conference, what questions can you ask the teacher that will cause them to reflect on their instructional practices?**

- Do you (the teacher) disaggregate student grades by gender, race, ethnicity, socio-economic status?
- What type of evaluative tool(s) are you (the teacher) using to determine if all students have mastered the material?
- What strategies/interventions are you using to engage your reluctant learners who may find it hard to be successful with traditional instructional strategies?

8. **What kind of data or research can you provide the teacher to direct them in the improvement of their instruction?**

The administrator should:

- Provide literature or research that will expose the teacher to awareness of how to educate multi-cultural learners (e.g. Ferguson's encouragement vs. demand).
- Suggest self-reflection on his or her own (teacher) data.
- Provide professional development opportunities and follow-up conversations.
- Interject the importance of relationship, relevance, and rigor.

Additional Considerations

Attending to the four areas of second-order change (culture, communication, order, input) remains an ongoing effort. Though each of the previous examples supports an organizational manner of promoting social justice advocacy, leaders for social justice advocacy must remember that this remains as much a personal process as it is a professional one. Therefore, leaders must be diligent in maintaining conversations that focus upon these issues.

With that in mind, the following activities will serve to promote and sustain growth of the professional staff:

- Circulate a particular article regarding racism and schedule a "think tank" for discussion.
- Form a student program: *Social Justice Leaders*, a middle school program in several school districts, has been most effective in creating a more inclusive school environment.
- Invite staff to share an evening at a movie that has a particular focus upon ending oppression.
- Use a fishbowl design with students to hear their voices regarding these issues.
- Create a book study group to share learning using various texts readily available to educators.
- Begin a parent program so that parent voices are honored and informed of school efforts.

Frequently seeking feedback from the staff regarding this journey is critical. As one final support for school efforts, *"Taking our Pulse"* was designed for middle schools that have been involved in this work over the past few years. It has been given at numerous times during the year, and results have been used to help focus upon continuing conversations and/or specific professional development areas. Teachers were asked to respond to these probes using a likert scale of 1 (not at all) to 5 (a great deal) regarding strategies and stance.

Strategies

Section 1: Planning instruction

1. I take time and effort to understand my students' backgrounds, cultures, interests, and life circumstances.
2. I include a wide range of tasks and activities to engage all of my students in the learning.
3. I ensure that my lesson is connected to my students' prior experiences.
4. I adjust my lesson planning in accordance with my students' cultural experiences and prior knowledge.

Section 2: During the lesson

1. I create a culture in which all my students' voices are respected (by me and their fellow students).
2. I treat mistakes as opportunities for learning.
3. I make clear to students my expectations for their learning.
4. I am explicit as to how my students can be successful.
5. I provide a variety of ways in which my students can demonstrate their learning.
6. During my teaching, to what degree am I conscious of my:

   Tone of voice?

   Distribution of my questions?

   Responses to wrong answers?

   Choice of words?

   Statements of encouragement?

   Statements of affirmation?

   Who I talk to the most?

   Who I talk to least?

   Who I engage formally?

   Who I engage informally?

Stance

1. I accept that my own unconscious disposition regarding racial difference impacts my teaching.
2. I recognize ways in which White privilege plays a role within our school.
3. I recognize ways in which some students are targeted.
4. I have had conversations with my colleagues as a way of understanding these issues.
5. I have seen changes in my own patterns of instruction as a result of this focus.
6. I feel that this professional development has been helpful to me as a teacher.

In the System

Countless research and texts have been published regarding system change, all of which provide reasonable suggestions, criteria, and considerations for this process. Much of this information is again focused predominantly upon cognitive changes, and as we have suggested treats the affective domain with less attentiveness. We believe system change must be promoted, supported, and reflected by leadership, and as previously stated, it is the affective domain that offers the greatest promise for this change. In *The Tipping Point*, Malcom Gladwell proposes three notions regarding change to be considered in this book (Gladwell, 2000). The first of these notions is the need for the support and endorsement of a few respected practicing school leaders. We believe that even a few voices that are earnest and genuine can begin to initiate a focus upon this kind of work.

In one district, the superintendent took an active role in the endorsement and support of this work. The district's social justice initiatives have had significant impact upon Black student graduation rates as they have increased from 70 percent to 84 percent in a three-year period. Culturally relevant teaching and leading is further reflected through student voice, in which the voices of all oppressed groups are honored and activated. A strong sense of belonging and community for all has been promoted that includes a view of difference as strength and contribution rather than deficit and the need for assimilation. School Board members have also participated in this courageous conversation, and subsequently established an Achievement Gap Committee which reports five to six times per year upon the progress toward excellence. The superintendent stated that:

"The social justice training provided by EEC has been life changing for myself and our district. We know each other better and we trust each other enough to talk about the hard things and to work together to find solutions that make our schools and our community a better place for children and adults."

A Case Study

A second condition for change is what Gladwell calls the "stickiness factor," one in which an idea, initiative, or product is exceedingly magnetic and compelling. Dr. Charlotte Ijei is the Director of Pupil Personnel and Diversity of a St. Louis Metropolitan School district and has been a central office administrator who has created a "stickiness factor" in this large district's system change. In 2007, this school district of the St. Louis metropolitan area began its journey with nine cohorts of administrators and teacher leaders (usually about twenty-five to thirty participants) attending a year-long program called Leadership and Racism. From 2007 to 2013 a total of twenty cohorts completed the program which represents over four hundred of the professional staff of the district. This is a large school district of 17,467 students of which 66.7 percent are White, 14.4 percent Black, 11.1 percent Asian, 3.8 percent Hispanic and 0.1 percent American Indian. Approximately 20 percent of the students are also eligible for Free and Reduced Lunches. The district also participates in the Voluntary Transfer program of St. Louis, Missouri, a state program which transports inner-city students, predominantly students of color, into this suburban school district.

This commitment for reform began a number of years ago when Dr. Ijei served on the Disciplinary Review Committee, a committee charged with the review of disciplinary actions that lead to either suspension or expulsion. While on this committee, she reviewed thoroughly the documents and forms used in the process, in particular looking at the language used within this information. What she uncovered was that disciplinary actions for students of color included language that suggested interpretation. Describing an act like pulling off one's earrings or dropping a book bag was used to support the idea that the student was "posturing for a fight." In other cases the term "fight" was associated with White students while terms such as "brawl," "riot," or "endangering safety" was used for students of color for essentially the same behavior. Benchmarking this differentiation in language therefore became a crucial reason for further study. Her superintendent at that time was in complete support of this further study and for this reason included the term "pluralism" in her official title. This term was another example of "stickiness" as it is seldom found in a central office title and would serve as a catalyst for discussion. It also allowed Dr. Ijei to broaden the scope of her social justice advocacy work to include not only race, but gender, age, heterosexism, and other "isms" that impact students within the system as well.

Dr. Ijei then created a small group of middle school students of color whose behavior patterns might have necessitated the more stringent results of either suspension or expulsion. Her thought was to work with these students, in particular regarding their sense of identity, so that these risky behaviors could begin to change. Working with this small group of eighteen students proved most effective as they demonstrated improved behaviors but, more importantly, improved instructional engagement. Thus, another "stickiness factor" emerged regarding this work because of the dividend it appeared to be having upon the district's achievement gap.

At this point the superintendent provided funding for the development of the Diversity in Action (DIA) teams. Under Dr. Ijei's leadership, the terms of *action* and *team* replaced the more commonly used terms of *review* and *committee* so often associated with diversity initiatives. Reframing this language, much as in the case of the word pluralism, was another way of creating a narrative regarding this work. The DIA teams would be a pro-active initiative in contrast to past efforts in this area that essentially were reactive in nature. Over the next few years, Dr. Ijei was able to create DIA teams in all of the elementary, middle, and high school buildings within the district. These teams meet quarterly in both areas served within the district and as well as in grade levels so that there is ample opportunity to compare ideas and activities used with the school settings.

While these activities were taking place with the professional staff, another example of this "stickiness factor," entitled Spirit of Excellence, was also growing in stature. The absence of students of color in advanced classes was troublesome and implied a lack of academic prowess. Therefore, Dr. Ijei began a small event with students of color and their parents. The idea for this program was to assemble students of color who were performing well in school and celebrate their efforts. In many ways this was an effort to confront the notion that doing well in school is merely "acting White." She was, in particular, working to give students of color, mentors and exemplars of academic success. The impact of this program grew from a small event in a local restaurant to hundreds of students and parents celebrating in the spring at the Blanche Touhill Performing Arts Center of the University of Missouri St. Louis.

The third and final condition from Gladwell's viewpoint is the power of context. Of course, the context of anti-racism efforts is often filled with struggle and confusion. Much of that confusion is the plethora of language used to describe this oppression. Admittedly, each individual brings his/her own unique experiences and idiosyncratic language to the conversation regarding racism. Finding common terms and essentially a shared language helps to minimize confusion and can focus more accurately upon the context for reform. Dr. Ijei's efforts, enlisting numerous participants in the courageous conversations provided by EEC, have been to provide a compelling reason for the conversations and actions. Of equal importance, this effort provided a shared language through which people could understand racism and all other forms of oppression at a deep level and participate as allies for change.

Further Conversations

With respect to school reform, Phillip Schlechty once suggested that we will need an aggressive change of the present system of public education. He suggested that the present system encourages, supports, and maintains the status quo and discourages invention (Schlechty, 1997). His description, almost twenty years ago, is alarmingly cogent with today's public education. Systems are ultimately built to stay the same. Therefore, this reform effort is without a doubt a formidable task for social justice leaders. Often in schools talking about race or any other form of oppression is avoided out of fear that it can be a volatile subject. The status quo thus remains in place. Social justice leaders must confront and address that which is oppressive and disenfranchises students. For this reason, social justice leaders need to serve as allies for one another. The leadership role they serve includes elements of isolation, overwhelming expectations, and few accolades for success. To build strength and confidence, continual opportunities to meet and share experiences should not be accidental but instead intentional. Chapter 6 of this book will look more deeply into how allies must be created for this social justice advocacy.

References

Bishop, R. S. (1990). Walk tall in the world: African American literature for today's children. *Journal of Negro Education*, 59(4): 556–565.

CREDE Standards for Effective Pedagogy (1970). Berkeley, CA: University of California. (CREDE Hawai'i is part of the national CREDE project.)

Ferguson, R. M. (2008). *Toward excellence with equity: An emerging vision for closing the achievement gap.* Cambridge, MA: Harvard Education Press.

Freire, P. (1970). *Pedagogy of the oppressed.* New York: Continuum Publishing Company.

Gladwell, M. (2000). *The tipping point.* Boston, MA: Little, Brown and Co.

Gorski, P. C. (2008). The myth of the culture of poverty. *Educational Leadership*, 65(7): 32–36.

Griffin, P. (2000). *Seeds of racism in the soul of America.* Naperville, IL: Sourcebooks Inc.

Johnson, D. W. and Johnson, R. T. (2009). Energizing learning: The instructional power of conflict. *Educational Researcher*, 38(1): 37–51.

Kendall, F., www.franceskendall.com

Kohl, H. (1967). *36 Children.* New York: New American Library.

Ladson-Billings, G. (1994). *The Dreamkeepers: Successful teachers of African American children.* San Francisco: Jossey-Bass.

Marzano, R. J., McNulty, B. A., and Waters, T. (2007). *School leadership that works: From research to results.* Alexandria, VA: Association for Supervision and Curriculum Development.

Mickelson, R. A. (2008). The persistent paradox: Race, gender, and adolescents' attitudes toward achievement. In J. U. Ogbu (Ed.), *Minority Status, Identity, and Schooling.* Charlotte, NC: Lawrence Erlbaum.

NCCRESt. (2005). *Equity in special education placements: A school assessment guide for culturally responsive practice,* Version 1. From http://www.nccrest.org

Nieto, S. (1996). *Affirming diversity: The socio-political content of multicultural education* (2nd ed.). White Plains, NY: Longman.

Perry, T., Steele, C. and Hilliard III, A. (2003). *Young, gifted and black: Promoting high achievement among African American students.* Boston: Beacon Press.

Postman, N. and Weingartner, C. (1969). *Teaching as a subversive activity.* New York: Dell Publishing Co.

Schlechty, P. C. (1997). *Inventing better schools.* San Francisco: Jossey-Bass.

Shields, C. M. (2004). Dialogic leadership for social justice: Overcoming pathologies of silence. *Education and Administration Quarterly,* 40: 109–132.

Steele, C. and Aronson, J. (1995). Stereotype threat and the intellectual test performance of African Americans. *Journal of Personality and Social Psychology*, 69(5): 797–811.

6 Allies: We Can't Do This Alone

> If unconscious pain is integral to the process of learning oppression then consciousness and healing are necessary in the process of liberation.
>
> (Bishop, 1994, p. 79)

As has been examined, our unconscious collusion regarding oppression of any kind is an integral process by which oppression is sustained. Our conversations are designed to bring a level of consciousness for those cast as members of the dominant group to recognize the manner in which privilege and superiority have been institutionalized. Similarly, we have shed light upon the ways in which internalized racism (oppression) becomes equally an unconscious thinking for those who have been targeted. For this reason we believe this work is an effort toward liberation. We also believe that this work cannot be done alone. Allies are critical for dismantling oppressions. A distinguishing characteristic of allies is their sense of power-with as opposite to power-over, their willingness to grasp deeply their own identity with neither shame nor hubris, their honesty, and their recognition that merely good intent cannot replace action. Becoming allies within our individual identity groups as well as between identity groups of others is a powerful alliance. As was the case with Bacon's rebellion, such an alliance will inevitably threaten the status quo. Working together "in serried ranks" is the *only way* to dismantle oppression.

Past Experiences

Our lessons began with a program entitled the Leadership and Racism Institute in 2001. It is from this program that we have constructed the template for creating these courageous conversations of the heart, head, and hands.

Dr. Phyllis Balcerzak, Associate Director of the Institute for School Partnership at Washington University in St. Louis, conducted a qualitative study to determine the impact this program had upon school leaders. The study was conducted to determine if the program's use of affective strategies at the retreat shifted the disposition and stance of participants toward their own confrontation of institutional racism and if shifts in consciousness transferred to changes in the school setting.

The study was a qualitative, longitudinal study of the impact of the program over a six-year implementation period. The summary data were comprised of an average rating on a five-point likert scale and comments written by participants on eight open-ended questions on the retreat and follow-up evaluations. This analysis included nineteen schools who participated in the program from 2003 to 2008. Dr. Balcerzak concluded that:

> The evidence from this study would indicate that the personal and public awareness and knowledge of racism created through the retreat program transferred to the educational setting as a desire among participant to act as change agents. Additionally, the strategies for change that are enacted vary from changing hiring practices, attending ally groups to share knowledge and practices, engaging colleagues in interpersonal conversation about racism in the setting and discovering ways to create learning.

Generally, comments on the retreat evaluation summaries were heavily weighted towards personal awareness/awareness of racism and a disposition to change one's relationships with colleagues around issues of race. For example, one participant stated that the experience was "powerful, shocking, challenging". Another said, "I am still digesting everything but know my eyes are open in a way they weren't before." And another, transferring awareness to a desire for personal change, committed to "Stop justifying myself." Others extended personal awareness to a desire for change in the broader social sphere: "I want to become aware outside of the retreat and use in real life, be the solution not the problem". And, "I want to connect with more people of the opposite race, develop my allies."

In response to prompts to specify post-retreat action steps, some responses indicated a specific school- or district-based act. A surprising number of responses to this question demonstrated a more affective disposition or stance to address racism which is not typically associated with job role in the educational setting. For example, although not directly asked, many respondents stated action steps to include working with others and affective relationship building within and across races within district teams. Therefore, we were pleased to see that the stance of participants to address racism, whether through more personal consciousness raising or "courageous conversations" with ally groups, emerged as a solid outcome of the program.

The follow-up evaluations, which include four full-day sessions, had the highest percentage of responses as a desire to enact strategic changes in the educational setting. These actions that resulted from individual shifts in consciousness appeared in a variety of ways. For example, in one district a superintendent immediately changed hiring practices to recruit candidates of color into leadership positions. In another, the administrator in charge of assessment began to analyze data in ways that would reveal inequities and remedies to the racial achievement gap. In a classroom, a teacher-designed instruction about racial inequities resulted in her class of predominantly White students writing letters to their city and state legislators about policy change. Another teacher, well-practiced in color-blind behaviors, pointed out to a student the similarity between a brown crayon and the color of her skin, resulting in the child's willing engagement in activities previously shunned. Nearly all of the respondents articulated a need for more time to talk with their ally groups.

The journey of liberating ourselves from oppressions must be diligently organized and result from collective action. To become allies is not merely a bond of friendship and mutual appreciation, although these attributes are, of course, desired in the relationship. Allies can be distinguished by the following characteristics:

- Their sense of connection to all people—Ubuntu ideology.
- Their lack of individualistic and ego centeredness.
- Their sense of process and change.
- Their willingness to embrace their own learning.
- Their openness and lack of shame about their own limitations.
- Their realistic sense of their own power or powerlessness.

One of our allies, Leon Sharpe, provides four behavioral aspects of working together in an authentic ally relationship. These behaviors can be most useful in constructing and sustaining the above characteristics.

Behavior #1: Awareness

To become an ally for one another begins with that personal journey of discovery as we have explored in the first two conversations. Trust must be present for this relationship to grow. The purpose of the fishbowl configurations in the previous conversation is to provide a tool from which trust can be built. As has been stated, the opportunity for each of the groups in their own racial identity to do their "work" in the presence of one another has been most instrumental toward building trusting relationships. Moreover, for both racial groups, this activity provides a "window" through which we see the difficulty, confusion, pain, and resistance that each of us encounter to liberate ourselves from oppression.

For this reason, it is important for Whites to recognize that the strengthening of allyship with People of Color is not just sensitivity about their targeting, but an understanding of the social, political, and personal power provided to Whites through the oppression. In Beverly Tatum's book *Can We Talk About Race?* her White ally friend, Andrea, provides a succinct description of that effort:

> In the end, I believe the issue is not how I respond to Beverly's Blackness. It is how I have come to understand my own Whiteness. I believe the issue for me is how I have come to understand social, political, and economic power and my unearned advantage and privilege as a White woman in a racist society. I believe the strongest thing that I bring to our friendship, our relationship, and our connection is an understanding of my Whiteness, something that for several decades, I was helped to not see or to not recognize its significance. It is my understanding of my own Whiteness, not my response to her Blackness that allows me to interact with Beverly in a way that continues to foster mutuality, connection and trust.
>
> (Tatum, 2007, p. 100)

Liberation cannot emerge from a righteous indignation toward the events that target and demean People of Color. Instead it must come from a personal effort on the part of many People of Color to work towards ridding themselves of what Dr. Joy DeGruy Leary describes as a "vacant esteem" (DeGruy Leary, 2005). She describes this as a state of believing oneself to have little or no worth, which is further exacerbated by the group and

White Privilege	*Internalized Racism*

societal pronouncement of inferiority. When society, community, and family influences confine individuals to a disparaging and limiting sense of identity this state of vacant esteem is inevitable. DeGruy goes on to note that vacant esteem is not a measure of one's actual worth. Once again a consciousness regarding the manner in which oppression is imposed upon those in subjection is the most effective tool for combating a vacant esteem. Self-esteem is enhanced with the recognition of not only one's inherent value, but the value that one brings to others.

Use Worksheet 6.1, with a prompt of: "How do you now see. . .", for continuing reflections that have begun with the conversations of the heart and head. After participants fill out this worksheet individually, have racial caucus groups form to once again promote deeper learning. Finish this activity with a full group conversation, which will once again build a sense of trust and respect as individual's share their reflections.

Behavior #2: Authenticity

Though authenticity seems a rather obvious behavior to expect from an ally, it may be more troublesome than folks may imagine. Once again, revisiting our personal identity development may be helpful in seeking a strong meaningful sense of authenticity. Peter Taubman provides another way of reflecting upon identity development, which he defines as three registers. He suggests that these registers lead to the construction, meaning, and function of identity. They are separate registers and emerge from different realities, and though they can be interactive, they provide each of us a compelling lens through which we can reflect upon "being real" (Taubman, 1993).

The first of Taubman's notions is that of the fictional register. He suggests that this emerges primarily as a construct of language, perceptions, and whatever stereotypes we might have learned about ourselves and others while growing up. This register is analogous to the "early years" of the cycle of socialization previously examined. This register in many ways imprisons us as subjects, which often leads to alienation and objectification.

> How we understand and come to know ourselves cannot be separated from how we are represented and how we imagine ourselves.
>
> (Giroux, 1997 p. 15)

Communal is the second register, and it emerges from group identification. It is in this register that we find our identity intertwined with others of "like" identity. This is the register that reflects some of the elements of the second cycle of socialization, that of institutions, i.e. political associations, faith-based communities, ethnic social spheres, fraternities, sororities, etc. This is a register that offers a broader view of self beyond individuality and it provides a sense of belonging and affiliation. This register can be homogeneous and boundaries for inclusion are specific. As such, this register can also carry misrepresentations and stereotypical frameworks.

The final register is autobiographical, which permits us to acknowledge that each individual has many "selves." It is a register that interacts with both the fictional and the communal. It is in this register that we elaborate, critique, and problematize, thus permitting license for our own idiosyncratic, unique identity. Often it is in this register that we experience dissonance as we confront the misrepresentation and stereotypic descriptions found in the first two registers.

As we begin to address our authenticity, use Worksheet 6.2 to deepen discussions among participants. Discussing these responses in a full group setting will assist participants in "being able to listen" and understand one another.

Worksheet 6.2 Registers of Identity

Fictional	Communal	Autobiographical

Behavior #3: Acuity

We live in a world of sound-bites where twenty-four hours of news programs fill our ears, often with shallow views of events that shape our world. Our sophisticated technologies arm us with tweets, chat-rooms, blogs, instant messaging, etc. which all work from limited space and words to elaborate, clarify, or illuminate life events. This new social network has no doubt many advantages regarding social change, and like all other technologies will continue to grow beyond its present format. However, it can substantially impact how fully we are able to access the complete story. As schools continue to seek and adopt more and more strategies for achieving success, social justice leaders must often grapple with an overwhelming set of data, initiatives, expectations, and standards that may or may not insure inclusive environments for all students. Thus a third behavior that enhances the role of an ally is that of acuity.

The word acuity is rooted in the Latin word *acuere* meaning to sharpen. Acuity is keenness of hearing, sight, or intellect. The role of an ally is to take time to look with greater clarity upon the numerous dimensions of any practice, policy, or nuance that promotes greater acceptance and inclusion of all students. Allies who serve each other are willing to ask the more difficult questions, elicit a variety of perspectives, and seek to discover what may be obscure and difficult to process. Thus acuity is to look beyond the obvious.

The Color of Discipline was research conducted by the Indiana Education Policy Center and funded by the Lilly Endowment, Inc. and Indiana University. This research abstract is a most useful document through which social justice leaders in schools can exercise acuity. Begin this activity by sharing Worksheet 6.3. Following the opportunity for each participant to read this abstract, conversations would then be used to stimulate the exploration of present school practices, classroom management, referral procedures, and other specific areas appropriate to this research effort. As in the case study found in Chapter 5, the data that can be accumulated with a PBIS program could easily be used to support these findings. Once again, the exercise is to examine information with greater acuity. This exercise is also consistent with critical race theory that is focused upon outcome and results of efforts toward enacting equitable policies.

Most professional staffs in the field of education seek civility and are by nature a congenial group. Efforts to improve our acuity regarding the learning environment will mean conversations must become collegial, courageous,

Worksheet 6.3 Research Abstract

Color of Discipline by Russell Skiba, Robert Michael and Abra Nardo (2000)

Disproportionate representation of minority students, especially African Americans, in a variety of school disciplinary procedures has been documented almost continuously for the past twenty-five years, yet there has been little study of the factors contributing to that disproportionality. Whether disparate treatment of a group can be judged as bias depends largely on the extent to which other hypotheses that could provide a credible alternative explanation of the discrepancy can be ruled out. In this study, investigation of three alternative hypotheses led to different conclusions for disproportionate representation based on gender, race, and socio-economic status.

First, racial and gender discrepancies in school disciplinary outcomes were consistent regardless of methodology, but socio-economic disparities appeared to be somewhat less robust.

Second, we found no evidence that racial disparities disappear when controlling for poverty status; instead, disproportionality in suspension appears to be due to prior disproportionality in referrals to the office.

Finally, although discriminant analysis suggests that disproportionate rates of office referral and suspension for boys are due to increased rates of misbehavior, no support was found for the hypothesis that African America students act out more than other students. Rather, African American students appear to be referred to the office for less serious and more subjective reasons.

Coupled with extensive and highly consistent prior data, these results argue that the disproportionate representation of African Americans in office referrals, suspensions, and expulsions is evidence of a pervasive and systematic bias that may well be inherent in the use of exclusionary discipline.

and at times, uncomfortable. Collegiality essentially would require of a social justice leader to argue profitability. Acknowledging and accepting the statement by Margaret Wheatley, "expect it to get messy at times", will help the conversation to remain authentic.

Behavior #4: Agency

Finding Our Voices

The need for allies to act as change agents is without question an expectation to be pursued. This work is ultimately about action and regardless of our racial identity we all have work to do.

> I have almost reached the regrettable conclusion that the Negro's great stumbling block in the stride toward freedom is not the White Citizens Councilor or the Ku Klux Klanner, but the white moderate who is more devoted to order than to justice.
>
> (Dr. Martin Luther King, Jr., *Letters from the Birmingham Jail*)

Speaking out and voicing a challenge from a White voice is usually not seen as argumentative or dismissive. Therefore, as a White ally, learning to use this privilege in ways to promote and create inclusive equitable environments for students is one measure of agency. Paulo Freire writes that true solidarity as an ally is a radical posture and characterized by "fighting at their side" to transform society (Freire, 1970).

The uncomfortable thought of being cast in the role of oppressor is filled with anguish and one can easily flee from such an identity. Learning to understand one's self as an oppressor means also to inherit an evil legacy, and is further made difficult by having never constructed that past. It means as well to recognize that the only way to understand the oppression is through the voices of those who have been oppressed. Ultimately it also means that the oppressed will know much more about the oppressor than the oppressor will know about the oppressed (Bishop, 1994). But this is the "role" created by the architecture of oppression. Moving beyond guilt and shame, emotions that do very little in terms of collective action and instead create inertia, must always be an exercise in listening without the need for defensiveness. No doubt there will be those so truly hurt by racism that their energy will feel like a personal attack. A White ally is one who will listen without the need to deny the experience, but instead seek more insight into how an oppressive system operates.

One does not need to sacrifice a sense of goodness to recognize the manner in which the system has placed one in the role of oppressor. White allies are those who have chosen to recognize the opportunity to contradict and challenge this role through action. This work is not to cause one to feel guilty about Whiteness, but instead to be critically conscious of how this singular characteristic can serve to interrupt the very system that creates it.

Feeling badly about one's Whiteness is a stage that many people experience. It's certainly not the goal of the educational process nor should

> it be the end point. Ideally, we should each be able to embrace all of who we are, and to recognize that in a society where race is still meaningful and where Whiteness is still a source of power and privilege, that it is possible to resist being in the role of dominator, or "oppressor" and to become genuinely antiracist in one's White identity, and to actively work against systems of injustice and unearned privilege.
>
> (Tatum, 2007, p. 37)

White allies are also those who challenge other Whites. Silence while in a predominantly White group when a racist joke is shared, a racial circumstance is denied, or an incident of oppression is minimized as merely an exception rather than a norm, is another source of collusion. A White ally knows also that "becoming genuinely antiracist" may also mean a breaking of ties with other Whites. Paradoxically, it might also provide permission and incentive for other White companions to do the same. White allies also are conscientious in their efforts to listen and not presume an understanding of what might be needed by People of Color. White allies do not seek leadership, but instead serve as resources to those Persons of Color who are called upon to lead. This is essentially the message of Freire for solidarity to be characterized as "fighting at their side." White allies are diligent in their efforts to learn, knowing full well that their ignorance is part of the oppression.

In the book *The Rebellious Life of Mrs. Rosa Parks*, Jeanne Theoharis gives a comprehensive history of the life and times of Rosa Parks, a truly courageous change agent. She begins the book with a description of the elaborate tribute following Mrs. Parks's death on October 24, 2005. She examines this event as a rewriting of the history of the Black freedom struggle along with Parks's own rich political history. Sadly, the fictional narrative of Rosa Parks as a seamstress merely too tired from work to give up her seat on the bus in Montgomery and by accident starting a significant civil rights movement for the entire country, continued to be the major focus of the pageantry of the October 24 event (Theoharis, 2013).

An ally of color is one who has accepted a much more precarious balance of both personal and public challenge. Raising one's voice as a Person of Color can be viewed dismissively and disregarded as merely a voice of anger and vindictiveness. Rosa Parks had a heightened awareness about her own power, her own rights and dignity, and her opportunity for success, and used her voice. The personal challenge for People of Color is to combat the feelings of futility and powerlessness. For Rosa Parks a respite from that sense of futility was experienced in the summer of 1955 when she attended the Highlander Folk School's program entitled Racial Desegregation: Implementing the Supreme Court Decision. Parks described this experience as fostering within her the following thoughts regarding People of Color and Whites as allies and the possibility of solidarity: "For the first time in my adult life that this could be a unified society, that there was such a thing as people of all races and backgrounds meeting and having workshops and living together in peace and harmony" (Theoharis, 2013, p. 39).

An ally of color is one who has come to believe that the reality of oppression is not a closed world with little chance of escape, but instead, as Paulo Freire writes, a limiting situation which they can transform (Freire, 1970). Therefore, the personal journey of an ally of color must be one of diligence in order to avoid the many traps that would cause one to think less of oneself. Joy DeGruy Leary describes this process as racial socialization in which efforts are constantly extended to keep informed and question the images People of Color are portraying of themselves. She encourages People of Color to examine the sounds and pictures we expose ourselves to and filter what news is heard, seeking truth (DeGruy Leary, 2005).

Let there be little doubt that to acknowledge and summarily dismiss the lies that seek to define allies of color is a daunting task. Because the socialization process is so embedded in the infrastructure of our society, there is little or no escaping the negative messages that swirl around People of Color throughout their lives. Yet, the personal and collective journey of shedding these limiting thoughts can be mitigated in a number of ways. One of those ways is through encouraging educators to promote a curriculum that shares the truth, not a marginalized truth, not a partial truth, but an authentic history that highlights the accomplishments and contributions made by People of Color. When this happens then young People of Color will have opportunities to see people like themselves in positions of authority. White students will also benefit as these are also the messages that confront the stereotypes.

A second way to diminish the repugnant narratives that permeate society relative to People of Color is to encourage White anti-racist folks to step up as powerful allies for People of Color. If we can join forces, and link arms in such a manner that we are working together to fight for justice "in serried ranks" then we can be assured of the promise of ultimate triumph, even when the field is assailed by forces of opposition (Lample, 1999).

Reflections upon Allies

With respect to continuing conversation, we have found that many of the quotes within this explanation of allyship create compelling discussions for participants. Here again is the opportunity for racial caucus groups (groups of similar race identity) as each has a unique obligation toward change. A full group discussion might begin with putting the quotes on flip chart paper and posting on walls. Inviting participants then to react to the quotes by writing their thoughts directly on the paper (or using sticky notes as an alternative) can lead to instructive and thoughtful dialogue. The facilitator's role in either of these possibilities is merely to promote inquiry among the participants to deepen their conversation.

Transference

All oppressions are built upon the power and privilege of a dominant group, believed to be superior, who also create a group that is targeted. When this occurs, many of those who are targeted will internalize the messages of inferiority placed upon them. With this in mind, any of the suggested activities can be easily adapted for other oppressions. For example, how can men be more aware of their own sense of power within the oppression of sexism? Conversely, how are women coopted by other women to gain advantage? How can perceived "straight" people become more critical in the examination of workplace policies that could target people of a different sexual orientation? How can Latinos strengthen an authentic relationship with other People of Color?

References

Bishop, A. (1994). *Becoming an ally: Breaking the cycle of oppression.* Halifax, Nova Scotia: Fernwood.

DeGruy Leary, J. (2005). *Post traumatic slave syndrome; America's legacy of enduring injury and healing.* Milwaukie, OR: Uptone Press.

Freire, P. (1970). *Pedagogy of the oppressed.* New York: Continuum Publishing Company.

Giroux, H.A. (1997). *Channel surfing: Racism, the media, and the destruction of today's youth.* New York: St. Martin's.

Lample, P. (1999). *Reflections on the individual, the institution and the community.* West Palm Beach, FL: Palabra Publications.

Skiba, R.J., Michael, R.S., and Nardo, A.C. (2000). *The color of discipline: Sources of racial and gender disproportionality in school punishment.* Bloomington, IN: Indiana Education Policy Center: Policy Research Report #SRS1.

Tatum, B. (2007). *Can we talk about race?* Boston, MA: Beacon Press.

Taubman, P. (1993). Separate identities, separate lives: Diversity in the curriculum. In L.A. Castenell, Jr. and W.A. Pinar (Eds.), *Understanding curriculum as racial text* (pp. 287–306). Albany: State University of New York Press.

Theoharis, J. (2013). *The rebellious life of Mrs. Rosa Parks.* Boston, MA: Beacon Press.

7 | **Lessons Learned**

For the things we have to learn before we can do them, we learn by doing them.
(Aristotle)

No Experts, Just More Experiences

As Aristotle suggests, it is in the doing that we have learned. With this in mind, we are not experts but we do acknowledge that we have a bit more experience in these essential conversations than most of our colleagues. That does not waive us from the same confusion, dissonance, struggle, and difficulties that we too encounter as we create and sustain our own racial consciousness. It has made us more mindful of the elements, conditions, and circumstances that can diminish at least some of that confusion, dissonance, struggle, and difficulties which emerges with conversations regarding oppressions.

Our work has always been about assisting individuals to see themselves and others through a different lens, one that discerns the thoughts, feelings, and motivations of those different from ourselves. A social perspective such as this essentially helps folks wear "others' shoes." The willingness to take this kind of social perspective has led to a number of behaviors which are of great benefit for educators working to create inclusive school environments. In a recent study of individuals provided opportunities to engage in social perspective training, the following results have great promise for the school settings. The researchers found the following outcomes:

- Participants stereotyped others less (Galinsky and Moskowitz, 2000).
- Participants improved their negotiation capacity: for teachers, this meant a stronger effort for compromises with students from backgrounds different from their own (Galinsky, Maddux, Gilin, and White, 2008).

- Participants responded less aggressively when provoked and showed an increase in altruistic behaviors (Batson, Early, and Salvarani, 1997; Batson, Sagar, Garst, Kang, Rubchinsky and Dawson, 1997).

This same research explored factors that might cause an individual to seek this kind of social perspective learning and found seven positive motivational factors (see Worksheet 7.1).

Our experience working with numerous participants from a multitude of various school settings aligns well with these motivational factors. We often find ourselves addressing the "choir" but recognize that even the choir needs to practice. To assume that everyone has begun this journey with any one or combination of these factors would be naïve. Thus, our experience has helped us to recognize the difference between *struggle* and *resistance*, two very different behaviors that all too often appear to be the same. When individuals become quiet, and remove themselves from the conversation, one could jump to conclude that this person is resisting. Behaviors that appear to be resistance may cause a facilitator to feel attacked or dismissed. The facilitator might become more insistent and even to some degree argumentative. Facilitative behavior of this type will only serve to "silence" the conversation.

Worksheet 7.1 Positive Motivational Factors

Motivational Factor	Description
High-stakes situations	Participants feel that a situation or circumstance is seen as especially important, e.g. high-stakes testing, increasingly diverse classroom settings.
Pro-social goals	A desire to help those that are targeted by the system.
Desire for situational knowledge	A desire to better understand and reduce the feelings of the uncertainty of others.
Relationship goals	Seeking to achieve, strengthen, or repair relationships
Social influence	A desire to gain cooperation, acceptance, and where appropriate compliance
Intrinsic interest	A feeling of curiosity and/or the need to understand.
Desire for self-knowledge	Seeking to understand self and how actions are interpreted by others.

This participant may be struggling and the withdrawal from the conversation might only be a search for some time. For this reason, give this individual that space, as in the use of a listening pair. We often share that we welcome struggle. Struggle, after all, is an element of learning. Developing a critical consciousness regarding oppressions involves dissonance. Announcing to our participants our appreciation of the struggles they might encounter may also give permission for others to indeed "struggle."

Our lessons emerged from a year-long program we created entitled the Leadership and Racism Program (LRP). The LRP program is designed with a two-day retreat and four additional full days of follow-up sessions. School leaders in this program consist of approximately twenty-five to thirty individuals representing teachers, administrators, and board members from a school district. The retreat is centered upon the personal issues of stance and includes the conversations of heart and head. The follow-up sessions, though not neglecting the personal journeys of participants, take a more active focus upon issues of strategy (the hands). For over a decade this program has been adopted by school districts in both urban and rural settings in several states. It has also served as our own personal "learning lab" for how to sustain this critical conversation of the heart, head, and hands.

Keeping Folks in the Conversation

There is no doubt that a conversation about oppressions and in particular racism is seldom one in which folks seek to engage. Clearly, our propensity to avoid this subject is seen in numerous arenas. It is no wonder then that we refer to this as a courageous conversation. Our experiences have been centered on the dual need to focus upon both content and process. As has been described earlier, part of the process must be the establishment of some guidelines for the conversation. Here again is where "oops" and "ouch" become strategies in which participants are able to stay in the conversation. Silence, after all, is the best friend of any oppression.

As in Chapter 1, Lisa Delpit shared the voices of individuals which benchmark some of the ways in which a conversation about racism is difficult. Each voice demands of us as facilitators to be exceedingly sensitive to the ways in which folks may want to escape or withdraw from the conversation. Often we ask folks to use their "I" voice as no one can speak for all members of their own racial identity. Therefore, we, too, choose to share the following lessons in our own "I" voices.

How Long?

As an African American woman who has facilitated healing conversations addressing the oppression of racism and internalized racism for close to three decades, I have come to realize that ridding oneself of the shackles that diminished a sense of self-worth is extremely difficult. Many people of color have been immersed and enmeshed in a pseudo reality of lies about our ability to walk in this world with a sense of pride and dignity for so long that it requires constant and intentional self-talk about our brilliance and nobility to withstand the daily onslaught of negative messages. When I have the opportunity to facilitate these powerful and emotionally laden experiences that lead to deeper and deeper levels of understanding of the severity of the wounds inflicted on the psyche of people of color by racism, I feel a sense of wonderment and awe at the tremendous coping strategies that people of color have put into play just in order to survive.

The unspoken question that often permeates the thoughts of members in the targeted group is: when will "it" end? Eventually that question is given voice by some of the participants. The "it" spoken of is the particular oppression, as well as the magnitude of the impact of that oppression. Often participants of color feel that the dire circumstances created by racism will never change. Because this sense of hopelessness can permeate the conversation, whether the oppression is racism, sexism, heterosexism, or any other form of oppressions, it is paramount that as a facilitator I share the many examples of resistance on the part of people to dismantle this oppression. The "how long" question that precedes that sense of hopelessness can be thwarted by participants acknowledging that there have been many people who have actively resisted the invalidation and exploitation of racism and/or other forms of oppression. It is also, for this reason, that we ask White people to do their work first in the fishbowl configuration. Observing White people struggling to understand their own participation in racism can lessen the feelings of hopelessness and futility for people of color. As facilitator it is necessary that I do my work of getting in touch with my feelings beforehand so that I can be as present as possible for the participants to express their emotions.

Joyous Celebration

Just as feelings of despair emerge as people of color share their own personal struggles more often than not, laughter and camaraderie will also prevail.

This feeling of connection among the members of the group is not hinged on personal relationships but on the phenomenon of fictive kinship, one in which oppressed people share an affiliation of history rather than blood. The group cohesiveness appears to give people of color the emotional fortitude to continue to work with other groups of color to tear down racial barriers. If this "liberatory" attitude is to persist, then groups have to be encouraged to continue to meet outside of this structured environment. Another lesson learned is that someone has to take the lead to convene the group so that the work of the group continues on this path of healing the emotional and psychological hurts. Unless this happens, participants who have worked so hard to shrug off some of the hurts of racism can find themselves entrapped once again by feelings of self-invalidation, self-recrimination, and self-doubt.

Compassion

Compassion is defined as a feeling of deep empathy and respect for another who is stricken by misfortune and the strong desire to actively do something about it. Compassion embodies the human quality of understanding (Germer, 2009). When facilitating this work, I remind participants that in order to eliminate or dismantle any oppression the virtue of compassion has to be cultivated not only for others but for themselves as well. When grappling with the throes of racism and internalized racism, there is a tendency to feel self-recrimination for past actions. Participants are remorseful because they were not discerning enough to know that they were operating out of the myth of inferiority that negatively impacted their relationships with other people of their own race. When comments are made that reflect this belief, I remind them that for centuries we have been given messages that have deliberately created disunity among us and that one of the most effective tools that we can use to eradicate this kind of thinking is holding ourselves in a place and space of self-compassion. Any act less will impede our progress and seriously limit our self-efficacy to become the social change agents that we are called to be.

And, finally, as a facilitator it is necessary that I do my work of getting in touch with those conscious and sometime subconscious places where I question my own self-worth, brilliance, and self-efficacy. When I do this beforehand, I can then be at my best as a facilitator of healing. I can be completely present for participants to express their emotions and realize their great potential to use their head, heart, and hands to dismantle any oppression.

Dr. Billie Mayo, Co-owner, Educational Equity Consultants

It's Like a Jungle Sometimes . . .

I identify as African heritage, U.S. born. In my experience, this identity alone brings with it a narrative that is often negative and questions the nobility of what it means to be a Black male in this country. A second identity that describes me is adjunct professor at a local university. In this capacity, I teach Cultural Diversity in the Media. In my class, students have the opportunity to examine all forms of media through the lens of diversity and inclusion. In my twelve years of teaching this class, both students of color and White students arrive at this conclusion: media, for the most part, portrays Black men as criminals, unintelligent, lazy, dead beat, and primarily entertainers in the world of sports and music.

I find that my engagement with Black men in other sectors of society such as the workforce, school, social organizations, church, and the gym to name a few, often centers around Black men feeling overwhelmed, hopeless, and exhausted from the micro aggressions encountered daily. One of my Black male students described his journey as a daily "walk through quick sand." My experience, as a Black man in this country is best described by a lyric in a 1980s song by Grand Master Flash: "It's like a jungle sometimes / It makes me wonder how I keep from going under."

In that *jungle,* silence for a Black man is the "unwritten" rule for civility. We are not able to express with any intensity the righteous indignation we feel when talking racism. Thus, often the anger, resentment, and pain we may feel must remain masked as to protect ourselves from the very false narrative that describes us. Approximately eight years ago, a very good friend of mine, challenged me to create a forum that would help to depressurize the experiences that many Black men live with daily.

We created *Black Men Speak Out,* a forum that provides a safe space for Black men to come together, to remind one another that we are smart, capable, and zestful men. It is a place to receive affirmation and reconnect with our innate goodness. We celebrate our hard work and the will to stay connected and remain in the jungle. We lift up brothers who may have gotten a promotion or an award of some type. We pray for brothers who may be suffering with a myriad of life difficulties that are often conflated with the negative narratives of Black men. We cry together when we hear or read about the senseless killing of yet another Black male. We continue to hold up the mirror that reflects our dedication to our children, our wives, our work ethic, and of course that Black Lives Matter.

Our time together provides a counternarrative to what we see, hear, and read, which is ubiquitous within this nation in all forms of communication. We meet monthly at my home on a Sunday and include dinner with our meeting. Thus, our conversations begin with breaking bread together, an age-old practice in numerous communities throughout the world. The nourishment of dinner then moves us into the facilitated conversation that I plan for the evening. As exemplified in this book, facilitating this courageous conversation must include some guidelines. We have only two: first, every voice counts and should be heard; and second, we leave this space *"better* than when we arrived."

In the eight years of hosting this forum we have had as few as fifteen brothers to over forty arriving at this gathering. On several occasions brothers who could not attend physically elected to call or Skype their participation. I recall one brother expressing his appreciation for such a space and describing our forum as the "man box," a place in which we could drop our masks, remove our armor, and be liberated from the labels, myths, and traps we negotiate every day of our lives. I describe our time together where handshakes and hugs abound, where love is felt, and we are each refueled to continue our lives.

In the fall of 2016, I and a few other brothers will initiate a group for gathering. Our intent is to meet quarterly as a book group, reading the literature that tells our history, the accurate one, the one we never read in school. We will select books that give each of us a stronger sense of ourselves, that provide us insight and energy to refute the insidious myths that surround and assault us every day. This is but one strategy vital for Black male survival. It is a reminder that in a country where we say freedom, justice, and liberty for all cannot be a "dream deferred," that one day, through our efforts, it will become a reality.

Anthony Neal, President/CEO, Educational Equity Consultants

Keeping White Voices in the Conversation

A few years ago a campaign to engage folks in a conversation regarding racism in a small city in Minnesota used a number of billboards that included a White woman or man with the following statement: "It's hard to see racism when you're White." The billboards were erected to promote a number of town hall opportunities to discuss the growing disproportionate figures involving poverty, unemployment, and health needs of minorities within the city. These billboards sparked a number of very angry White people who believed they were being accused of being racist. This anger led to threats waged against the mayor to remove the signs. Needless to say, the possibility of a courageous conversation was scuttled by White people angry with the billboards regardless of the intent. I believe, as a White male, this episode reflects a few ways in which staying in the conversation for White people is a challenge.

Racist vs Racism

No doubt the word racist carries as much baggage for White people as does the "n" word for People of Color. The word alone can spark, as in that small town in Minnesota, an uncomfortable array of feelings that do little to encourage or enhance a thoughtful conversation regarding racism. The term racist for White people is yet another example of Delpit's description of silencing the dialogue. I often grew mute when hearing this term. My desire in the past had been to attempt to prove I was not a racist. My arguments and proofs of that fact often only complicated the conversation. For People of Color hearing me list the ways in which I was not a racist, merely exemplified my naivety regarding the real issues of racism. It also placed me in a defensive posture, and as always, if one takes a defensive posture one will likely need it. Though my intent was to extract my identity from such an alarming descriptor, this only created an impact upon People of Color of my unwillingness to continue the dialogue.

Race is clearly a social construct and most everyone knows this fact. To keep Whites in the conversation, I have learned to move people away for the term racist to instead an exploration of how we, as Whites, are cast in the role of the dominant player of structural racism. Like numerous White people this is not the role that we chose, only one of circumstance of birth. Consequently, through no fault of our own, our "lot had been cast" within the oppression of racism; this circumstance, as with privilege, in the words of Harry Brod, is not something chosen and, therefore, able to be given back. Helping White people to move away from the immediate need to distance themselves from the term racist and, instead, inviting a conversation to examine racism appears to keep people in the conversation. It would also be applicable for any other form of oppression that relies upon the "ist" terminology.

Don't Have the Words

It seems quite unfortunate that the kind of vocabulary and conversation that rolls off of the tip of the tongue for People of Color regarding racism is not very accessible for White folks. My own experience as a child was that racism was never discussed at the dinner table nor was the reality of my White identity. When discussed, though rarely, racism became a narrative of Black people behaving badly and thus racism was simply individual acts of meanness by People of Color. I was a young White boy and with some exceptions behaved reasonably well and never with a thought of hate or meanness. So how could I be part of racism? My early years never informed me of the oppression of racism and absent of any racial experiences meant that talk about racism became troublesome and awkward. Seldom did a conversation about racism begin with the question of "What does it mean to be White?", and all too often the conversation therefore became what it meant to be "not" White. The subtle idea that racism was a Black problem became embedded in my thinking and excused my voice from the conversation. So I thought.

Like numerous other White people, I had very little language with which to explore my own participation in the oppression of racism. The fish-bowl, though difficult, is truly the opportunity for us as White folks to find a language from which we can explore our participation in structural racism. In that language we do however, encounter yet another word for which we struggle. The word that is essential for a thoughtful conversation regarding racism is privilege, and like racist, it can also silence the dialogue.

Privilege . . . Not Me!

It is not uncommon for Whites to confront the idea of privilege with a fair degree of skepticism and in some cases, anger. Over the years of doing this work, I believe that reactions of this nature usually emerge from folks because of three characteristic that have become analogous to privilege. The first of these is elitism. The elite are often felt to be people "above" the masses, a very small group of individuals who stand ready to judge others as unworthy, incapable, and of little value. In this manner, the elite have a kind of superiority that sets them aside, affording them a certain level of status within the society. This status serves once again only to benchmark the divisiveness of oppression. Few of us as White people want to be regarded as participants in this elite group. Privilege has also become analogous with "cheating the system." Those who have privilege are able to distort the rules, change the game, and of course all of that for their own advantage. Obviously a certain moral prerogative is violated when one "cheats" and again, as a White man, that is not the image I would like of myself. Finally, a third and the most accessible element ascribed to privilege is materialism. As discussed in previous chapters, plenty of White folks have struggled with poverty and disenfranchisement, but even this does not negate other sources of privilege. Benefit of doubt, assumptions of capability, mobility, and for the most part the opportunity to choose our challenges may not be regarded as materialism but are indeed issues of privilege. After sharing these three elements, I will often suggest that it is a bit of a paradox that perhaps another of our privileges is to even create these arguments against privilege.

"Good White Person"

Staying in the conversation is often viewed by White people as evidence of being the "good White person." This, too, has a paradoxical element. This benchmark of "goodness" does not automatically equate to understanding. Instructive conversations regarding racism will often for White people surface their own cluelessness. For many White people, living in a bubble has denied us exposure and experiences that help us recognize structural racism. The fish is the last to discover the ocean. Thus, being a good White person is often only in the context of individual behavior. Helping each other, as White allies, must be an effort to act, to confront, to challenge each other. It is in the flexing of privilege to change that we must define our "goodness."

Dr. Phil Hunsberger, Co-owner, Educational Equity Consultants

Participant Voice

In one school district for which we have worked, an outside evaluator was hired to explore the impact upon individuals regarding these courageous conversations. The evaluation was conducted in 2012 and used survey and focus group strategies to gather evidence. Eighty-eight employees participated in the program representing a 44 percent return, a statistically reliable percentage. Eighteen teachers and administrators were involved in two focus group activities. Ideally, a focus group would include a greater sampling size, but feedback from this strategy was still considered valid and helpful for providing an understanding of the program's strength.

When asked of teachers in the focus groups the greatest strength of the program, responses included the following:

- The ability to hear other perspectives.

- The strength of the dialogue and the deep learning.

- The content and delivery given the difficulty of the materials and emotional paradigms encountered in this challenging discussion.

- The honest dialogue and the facilitators' honoring of each person's perspective.

- The historical background provided and that most non-minority participants were unaware of the systemic effects and subtle infrastructures within racism.

When asked of administrators in the focus groups the greatest strength of the program, responses included the following:

- The program enabled and encouraged dialogue that would likely not have taken place otherwise.

- The facilitators created a safe place to have the conversation.

- The activities pushed participants out of their comfort zones and gave them a common language.

- The history of systemic racism mirrored teacher comments that systemic influences in education today had not been considered.

The survey results indicated that 81 percent of respondents either agreed or strongly agreed that the anecdotal discussions were helpful in understanding the systems and beliefs that affect race relations. When asked about engagement during the training, 83 percent agreed or strongly agreed that they were fully engaged. Asking respondents as to whether the training shed new light on many of the unintended elements that hinder positive race relations, 90 percent agreed or strongly agreed. When asked if they agreed with "I would recommend this training for all faculty and staff of this school district," 100 percent of teachers and 88 percent of administrators agreed or strongly agreed.

The report also included these voices with regard to the program:

- "I thought I was 'enlightened,' but realized I had a lot of work to do."
- "This was an awesome experience. Since the program, my class and I have had many rich conversations which are no longer uncomfortable to have."
- "This program had a huge impact on the teachers in my building that attended."
- "This was without a doubt the best professional development opportunity I have ever had."
- "It was amazing and life changing. Necessary and relevant."

Finally, one comment that likely has been the motivation for this book:

"This has been one of the MOST valuable experiences in my educational career. I am fascinated by the data presented and am struggling to know how best to disseminate this information to the remainder of my staff. I would LOVE to continue the conversation of how to educate our peers in a thoughtful and meaningful approach."

Final Thoughts

The notion of final thoughts surely only applies to this manuscript. A final thought that would somehow eradicate racism and all other forms of oppression would indeed be a magnificent conclusion. Instead it is our hope that this book has provoked in the reader a desire to create a conversation of the heart, head, and hands for themselves as well as others. That the reader be willing to *Keep on Keeping On*. For with respect to dismantling racism or any other form of oppression, we are reminded of the African proverb that says:

After the Mountain, More Mountains.

References

Batson, C. D., Early, S., and Salvarani, G. (1997). Perspective taking: Imagining how another feels versus imagining how you would feel. *Personality and Social Psychology Bulletin*, 23: 751–758.

Batson, C. D, Sager, K., Garst, E., Kang, M., Rubchinsky, K., and Dawson, K. (1997). Is empathy-induced helping due to self-other merging? *Journal of Personality and Social Psychology,* 73: 459–509.

Galinsky, A.D. and Moskowitz, G. B. (2000). Perspective-taking: Decreasing stereotype expression, stereotype accessibility and in-group favoritism. *Journal of Personality and Social Psychology,* 78: 708–724.

Galinsky, A.D., Maddux, W.W., Gilin, D., and White, J.B. (2008). Why it pays to get inside the head of your opponent: The differential effects of perspective taking and empathy in negotiations. *Psychological Science,* 19: 378–384.

Germer, C. (2009). *The mindful path to self-compassion: Freeing yourself from destructive thoughts and emotions.* New York: The Guilford Press.

Made in the USA
Las Vegas, NV
15 July 2022

51582370R10079